UPSIDE
DOWN

HOW TO REVERSE YOUR
THINKING TO CREATE
EMOTIONAL FREEDOM

UPSIDE DOWN

HOW TO REVERSE YOUR THINKING TO CREATE EMOTIONAL FREEDOM

GLEN HONG, Psy.D, MSW

London

Upside Down: how to reverse your thinking to create emotional freedom

The book information is catalogued as follows;
Author Name(s): Glen Hong
Title: Upside Down: how to reverse your thinking to create emotional freedom
Description; First Edition

1st Edition, 2021

Book Design by Leah Kent

ISBN 978-1-913479-89-3 (paperback)
ISBN 978-1-913479-90-9 (ebook)

Published by That Guy's House
www.ThatGuysHouse.com

This book is dedicated to anyone who is seeking emotional validation and understanding for everything that they feel because everyone deserves that right.

CONTENTS

Foreword

I remember twenty years ago while I was in my twenties with no job and not sure what to do with my life, I was sitting on my couch aimlessly flipping through the various channels on the television. During that summer, *The Oprah Winfrey Show* began "Change your Life TV" and the very first episode featured John Gray, who was teaching about the four basic emotions that people feel. That first episode opened the door to exploring the importance of my own feelings. Later that extended to other self-help specialists like Iyanla Van Zant, Gary Zukav, Marianne Williamson and many others who explored the greater meaning of life, and this set the foundation for me to see myself and my life in a different light. I would watch that show religiously, and I literally was another daytime devotee along with the many housewives who would make that show an essential part of their day at that time. On one particular episode when Iyanla was on the show, she looked directly into the camera and said, "To all the housewives at home, you are a beautiful flower!" And when I saw that I remember yelling back at the television, "Yeah, I am a beautiful flower!" while my good friend who was next to me looked at me perplexed and said, "What the fuck is wrong with you?" However, at that point, I did not care because I knew that my life's direction was about to change. That show was the starting point that gave me permission to see life differently and to choose a different path than the unconscious way that I was living. And shortly after, I began my journey into the field of mental health, going to graduate school studying both the fields of clinical psychology and social work, teaching clinical courses at a university setting, as well as providing counseling services to all demographics ethnically and socio-economically. I have worked with the homeless population, suicidal clients, the chronically and severely mentally ill, as well as with affluent and well-to-do individuals who were thriving in their particular field. And in this journey of helping others, as well as trying to understand my own life, I experienced this expanded space of seeking to understand the spiritual components of life, as well as understanding the clinical components which I was trained to do, along with everything in-between. And my soul purpose and interest became the mental, spiritual, and emotional space where the various components overlapped, and commonality could be seen. Through this journey, I would ask questions when it came to spiritual concepts that were not rational, and would question the medical model when life went beyond rationales. This book is the result of that twenty-year exploration. It is the overlapping knowledge as well as my own personal under-standing about how to deal with yourself through your emotions, and to live on the terms of your success, and not based on the pains of your past and the perceptions of others.

Throughout this book, I reference clients sharing a little bit about their stories, and it seems like I am not sharing my story at all. However, this book throughout is my story because each prin-ciple and construct represent every lesson that I have learned based upon the various settings and stages of my life. It is how I choose to see the world and how I eventually decided to live. The understanding of the sympathetic structure is my stored pain from all of the people in my life that told me that I was no good and that I would amount to nothing, as well as those that tried to get me to conform to what they thought I should be. It is also the stored pain and my complete ownership for all of the self-sabotaging choices that I made in my life while living in a sympathetic survival state and experiencing the same repetitive disappointing cycles over and over again. And the parasympathetic structure is the activation of my desires and giving myself permission to break free from living in a survival state and start living the life that I always wanted to live. It is the activation of me choosing my dreams, my passions, and honoring the emotions that are within me over seeking to avoid my pains of the past by prioritizing my rationale. It is the activation of me letting go of the individuals in my life who did not have my best interest, setting boundaries with those who believe that they had my best interest, and opening the door to those that genuinely do have my best interest. It is the activation of me no longer trying to convince myself of my worth through repetitive thinking and honoring myself by treating my feelings as if they are worthy all on its own. And finally, the parasympathetic structure is the choice to no longer apologize and ask for permission to be self-full and ultimately honor the creation that is ME! Simply put, I am living an upside-down life!

Chapter 1

The Reason for This Book

During my time working in a private practice setting, I remember working with one client who I will name Jim. He was seeing me for his primary symptoms of depression and secondary symptoms of anxiety. Jim was working at a job that he did not want to be in, and he was doing his best to maintain his life for his two children and his wife. He was also having marital problems as he felt unappreciated in the marriage, and he shared that he had difficulty communicating his needs to his wife. Jim was constantly on edge and had a negative view of every area of his life. I had seen him for three sessions, and he was getting moderately better, but something changed during the fourth session. When he came into the session, Jim was very startled and had a very tense look on his face. I quickly brought him into the office and had him sit down and discuss what was going on. He shared that his body was tense and that his heart was beating very fast because he was just in a near-fatal car accident. As he was sharing the story, he described how when he was making a left turn when the signal turned green, a car went on a red light on the opposite side, and then he completely swerved to avoid hitting the car. He also shared how the car continued to slide and that he had to break very hard in order to avoid hitting another car. While this was happening, another car from the diagonal side slammed on the brakes as he almost hit him directly on his driver side.

As he shared this story, he described how he went into this fight-or-flight mode as he reacted quickly to avoid hitting the car and at the same time went into a frozen response when his body could not move as the oncoming car was close to hitting him. The man was visibly shaking, and his voice was trembling as he shared his story. He also discussed how after the event ended, he was thinking about all of the worst-case scenarios that could have played out while coming to the clinic to see me, and that he was hesitant to come because he wanted a guarantee that he would be safe when arriving. As he shared and processed all of this with me, Jim's body continued to shake for a while, and he began processing his fears when it came to his life, the aspects of his life that made him angry, as well as the indecisiveness that had dominated his actions. After about forty minutes of processing, Jim stopped shaking and had an expanded look on his face. He began to smile, and he shared how he had no anxiety or depressive symptoms at all. Jim added, "I have been in therapy for years, and I have never felt this good in my life!" He continued on, sharing how he was going to talk to his wife after he got home from this session, and start looking at his future more seriously, and live the life that he always wanted to live. I felt bad that Jim had experienced a near-fatal car accident, but I was also happy for him that he was feeling such joy and elation after the event ended, and that he was going to use this incident to do things that he was hesitant to do before.

Jim continued to see me after, and for two consecutive weeks, he shared how he was extremely happy and grateful for his life, and that he even discussed and shared his true feelings with his wife, which he had not done in years. Jim was also planning on looking for a new job and transitioning into a work setting that he believed would be healthier for him. He explained how he had no depressive symptoms and little to no anxiety symptoms at all. He said that he felt a greater mental and emotional expansion and that anything was possible in his life. When I asked him what has changed about him, he answered simply, "That life-threatening event and the processing after took away all of the pain and suffering that I felt inside. It was as if these bricks in my stomach and head had been permanently removed." I was so impressed with Jim's progress and amazed at how quickly this change occurred for him. However, when Jim returned the following week, he shared that he did not follow up in doing job interviews elsewhere, that he started shutting down when it came to communicating with his wife, and that he reverted back to his old behaviors. Jim's depression returned as well as his anxiety symptoms. When I asked him why he thought he went back, he shared, "The momentum and the freedom I had for three weeks slowly started to go away, and I started to feel like life was dangerous all over again. It was as if that really strong person never existed." It was during this time that I saw a correlation between the life-threatening event he experienced, his sympathetic nervous system, and his overall outlook on life. I wanted to understand how he had gone from living his best life for three weeks after the near-fatal event and the activation of his nervous system, to then going back to his previous level of functioning when he began treatment. I also wanted to understand what it would take for Jim to live in that higher level of functioning repeatedly versus staying in his baseline level of depression and anxiety. I knew at this point that the nervous system was involved, and I started seeing depression and anxiety through a different lens. This was the entry point to the treatment that I am laying out for you in this book.

The Sympathetic Nervous System

The sympathetic nervous system, which is part of our reptilian brain, is also known as your fight-or-flight response, which is activated whenever you are in a life-threatening situation. This reptilian system is part of your central nervous system, and when a dangerous situation occurs, the body goes into a protective and reactive response. The sympathetic neurons of the spinal cord communicate with the peripheral sympathetic neurons via a series of the sympathetic ganglia, and then it goes into a fight, flee, or freeze predicament in order to seek survival. For example, if someone held a gun to your head, your nervous system would automatically go into a fight, flee, or freeze response. The options would be to fight the individual through domination, flee the situation through escape, or freeze, playing dead in hopes that the gunman would not pay any attention to you. While the body is trying to figure this out, the mind would be racing thinking of all possible scenarios, your body would tense up, your heart would beat fast, and you would have shortness of breath because your body would need to react quickly. Also, your body would try to mind-read what the gunman would be thinking in order to come up with the perfect response because one wrong outcome could mean life or death. In this scenario, if we break this down, your own ego response would engage in the following:

- going into a negative filter of thinking where only the worst-case scenarios of your life are being played out

- placing dependency on outer circumstances, even trying to mind-read what another person is thinking because you are completely helpless

- not making any decision because an immediate and perfect outcome is needed because, literally, your life is on the line.

The purpose of this system is to not make you happy, but the whole goal is to keep you safe. In order to be safe, the system only focuses on the negative possibilities that can occur because survival is its primary purpose. Once the sympathetic system knows that the body is safe, it will release itself and allow the mind and body to expand to focus on being happier. When I thought about my client Jim more, I realized how his reaction when he faced his life-or-death situation mirrored his experience when it came to his overall quality of life. Whether it was his accident or whether it was addressing his issues at work, Jim would go into a negative filter of thinking only thinking about the worst-case scenarios. He would not entertain any possibility that his life could get better. He would often go into intense anxiety attacks trying to mind-read what his co-workers were thinking about him, assuming that all his co-workers hated him. And he was constantly feeling like he was at the mercy of his own environment. In his daily life, Jim was constantly living in a protective and reactive manner. The other aspect of Jim's life that correlated was that he often froze when it came to making decisions related to his work or with discussions with this wife, just like if he had a gun to his head. Jim, during sessions, would often make statements like "My boss is going to kill me," and "I had a disagreement with my wife, and my life is now over!" Even though Jim's life was not in danger when it came to his own quality world, he was living as if he were. The key was figuring out how he could release himself from his perceived quality-of-life dangers to living in freedom once again.

Similarly, when I spoke at an event to young graduate social work students in a university setting, I was able to see the sympathetic nervous system in action. The two speakers before me were sharing the struggles of being a social worker and detailing that this job is a calling because of the struggles that you will have to endure. When it was my turn to speak, I shared how social work had lower salaries than most professions but given all of the opportunities that are available in the field, that within five years of graduation from their master's program, that they have the opportunity to earn a six-figure income. I was also sharing how there is flexibility in terms of being able to make your own schedule, and that myself and other colleagues juggle two or three jobs with various hours to maximize our opportunities. My goal was to promote an encouraging message that you can work in this field, help others, and at the same time live a good life yourself.

When I made that statement, students and faculty began raising their hands making statements like, "How dare you tell me that money is the most important thing in the world when it comes to social work!" Other statements included, "I am offended that you are saying working one job is not good enough and that I have to work more. How dare you!" It went on as one of the faculty staff shared, "Most get into social work because they themselves grew up in poverty, and so for you to make these callous statements shows that you are tone-deaf." One student also shared, "I will only believe you if you can guarantee that this is going to happen for me, or else your message is just fake news." I listened to each statement and responded by sharing that my goal was not to offend anyone, but to show that you can help others and at the same time, maximize your income in the process.

I was perplexed because I thought this reaction would be warranted if I had made a statement like, "You will never make it in this field, and you all suck!" Some students began to cry and a few more shared how they did not get into social work for the money and that this was hurtful. After I was done speaking, one of the university faculty spoke to me privately, telling me that they got what I was trying to say, but that I should lower the expectations of my message because it was offensive. That staff member told me directly, "We all know social work is about being poor and so that message does not relate." I looked that faculty member right in the face and asked, "You are telling me that my message of 'You can be successful financially and emotionally in the field of social work' is offensive?" and she shook her head yes, saying, "I can't believe that you do not see it." It took me a while to process that event and to come to terms with what had taken place.

At that point, I realized that whether it was Jim in that near-fatal car accident or in his daily life avoiding what he really desired in his heart, or the social work students who were fighting the message that you can have it all when it came to the profession, the sympathetic nervous system was involved. It was at this point that I saw how the sympathetic nervous system not only goes into a protective response in life-or-death situations to promote physical safety, but it is also used when it comes to one's emotional safety as well. From an emotional standpoint, opening your heart and seeking your dreams and desires is perceived as being just as dangerous as having a gun to your head and possibly losing your life. In both cases, quality of life is thrown out the window, and survival and protection becomes the primary goal. This is why most people live their life just trying to get by or lowering expectations because of the fear of disappointment. In the sympathetic world, disappointment is the same as death. The key to getting out of this sympathetic response then is to allow the body to see that seeking your desires and dreams are actually safe. This can then open the door to being released from the emotional prison that people are living in and allow healing to take place in a more rapid and effective manner.

Once your sympathetic nervous system becomes a part of your emotional quality world, it cannot differentiate a physical danger versus being emotionally hurt, and the approach to coping is the same. You will go into a spectrum of the fight, flee, or freeze reaction, and your core decision-making will be based upon isolation and safety. How many times have you self-sabotaged your own success? How many loving and caring people have you pushed away while keeping around individuals who continue to hurt and diminish you? How many times have you went against your greater self and chose to continue to stay in the same mediocrity? All of these actions are the sympathetic nervous system infiltrating your emotional life and leading you to choices of being alone.

The reason is that isolation is the ultimate form of safety, whether it be your physical or emotional world. The primary emotions that dominate you in this safety state are anger, fear, and indecision, the reason being that these emotions are the by-product of your fight, flee, or freeze response. Once you are fully immersed in this sympathetic level of living, the mind is in a continuous negative filter, negating any possibilities that life can get better; the body is in a helpless state believing that you are at the mercy of your own environment, and your overall being is living in a reactionary and protective response where you will not pursue your life goals unless a guarantee of safety can be promised.

A Traditional Approach

When it comes to the treatment of depression and anxiety, a traditional treatment approach is to go from the top down, meaning that you focus on a person's thoughts first, and if you change their thoughts, this will change the persons' feelings, and from there that will change their actions. A typical example of this is the approach known as cognitive behavioral therapy or CBT. The approach is focused on using rationale and facts when it comes to addressing your emotions with the goal of establishing more intellectual control of your emotional processes. This is a problem-solving approach where each perceived problem is dissected circumstance by circumstance, and you work with a therapist to solve each and every single problem. It is a very mind-focused approach, and the goal is to not only fix the perceived external problems but to change how you perceive these situations so that they can be viewed in a more rational way. In therapy, therapists will often make comments about emotions like, "They can be highly irrational," and, "Using your emotions to guide you is setting yourself up for failure." In fact, using your emotions as a guide to decision-making is termed as an unhealthy coping skill known as *emotional reasoning*. Usually, therapists will schedule to see a client weekly and assign homework. The homework usually consists of keeping a log of their thoughts, feelings, and actions, and each week, the various situations of their life are explored. The goals of a traditional therapy approach are to:

- be in a problem-solving mindset and fix the various areas of one's life that need to be solved

- be more rational when it comes to

addressing your emotions

- set up realistic and reasonable goals that can be achieved.

Over time, the goal is to be more rational when it comes to your own emotions, and success means that your intellectual guidance system takes over and has more authority than your own emotional guidance system when it comes to addressing your life. I provided this approach for many years to clients, and when a person became more rational, and when an individual showed more dominion over their emotions because of their mind, success was being reached. The emotions of an individual could be better controlled and understood as long as the mind and the thought process became the central focus. More often than not, this allowed an individual to be more accepting of their life, and the focus of small changes became the priority. This would be great for the most part until a deep emotional response of anger, fear, or indecisiveness would happen, either randomly or triggered by an event that occurred, and the containment of emotions through the mind would not work for the client. When these outbursts of emotions happened, it was almost always related to the desire of the client to have greater self-actualization and to seek a goal that went beyond the rationalization of the mind. One client I knew would often get really angry every few months and state, "I really want to have my own business, but I know that this is a pipe dream!" Often times, the desire would be identified as unrealistic to the client and a comment like, "I am just being irrational, and my emotions are getting the best of me," would be the response. The goals and desires shared would be outside of the comfort zone of the client, and it would extend beyond the structured and contained life that was being lived. Over time, however, it was these specific moments that could be identified as irrational from a traditional standpoint that were actually the opportunities to break away from the sympathetic response and unleash the true potential of the individual. The key was to break out of the contained negative filter of danger and transition to safety, meaning going from the sympathetic nervous system to the parasympathetic state.

The Parasympathetic System

The opposite of the sympathetic nervous system is the parasympathetic nervous system, which works together in order to promote a proper balance of the body. The parasympathetic nervous system is the division of the nervous system that controls largely the automatic processes such as digestion, respiration, and heart rate. It acts in concert with the sympathetic nervous system and conserves the body's energy by bringing bodily functions back to homeostasis, particularly after the fight-or-flight response is activated. Once this balancing act occurs from sympathetic to parasympathetic, it opens the door for the mind and body to gather information by calming the body and becoming more openly available to potential and possibilities. That is why when a dangerous situation occurs and then the situation is over, the body will go from a fight, flight, or flee response to a tonic response of freedom and joy, because the nervous system went from the sympathetic to the parasympathetic. When the parasympathetic nervous system is activated to balance the sympathetic nervous system, the body becomes more:

- open and available to receive information due to a calmer mind

- emotionally expressive as communications of feelings become easier

- available to explore the possibilities of one's life as tonic chemicals are released.

Without the parasympathetic nervous system, the monitoring and regulation of everyday body processes would be impossible. If the sympathetic nervous system becomes overactive and promotes imbalance with the parasympathetic nervous system, an increase of symptoms can occur, such as cardiovascular disease, chronic heart failure, and hypertension. Just one boost of sympathetic signaling raises the blood pressure, which may cause hypertension. In short bursts, the body's physical stress response can be useful by granting an energizing boost of mental focus. However, if prolonged, the stress signals whizzing through the body will wreak havoc, and the constancy of stress will increase blood pressure and promote a build-up of fat.

The parasympathetic nervous system plays a vital role in maintaining both mental and physical health by helping the body to calm down from stress reactions that elevate blood pressure, cause pupil dilation, and divert energy from other body processes to fighting or fleeing. It has been chronicled in various neuroscience journals that sympathetic dysfunction underlies mental health conditions such as anxiety, depression, and chronic stress and that increased parasympathetic activity is essential in alleviating these symptoms. When the parasympathetic system takes over your central nervous system, the survival and reactive components subside and proactive responses occur, allowing the mind and body to develop greater meaning and purpose in one's life. This activation allows for an individual to focus on their own quality world and to identify how to live the life that they want.

When working with Jim, he was having moderate changes when it came to his depression before his accident, but afterwards, he was functioning at a much higher mental and emotional level. That was because instead of mentally processing the event first from a top-down approach, he went from an upside-down approach focusing on the nervous system first. In successive therapies after Jim went back to his baseline functioning of depression and anxiety, through nervous system processing using an upside-down approach, he was able to repli-cate the outcomes he experienced for three weeks after the car accident on a daily basis.

The Upside-Down Approach

The upside-down approach differs from the top-down traditional approach in that it focuses less on your mind and more on your nervous system processing. A traditional top-down approach, as stated before, starts from your thoughts, which then create your feelings and then your actions. In this method, rational thinking is key and establishing intellectual dominion over your emotions is the primary goal. In this non-traditional upside-down approach, we start from your nervous system processing first, then transition to your emotions, and lastly move to the top, focusing on your mind. From this perspective, the nervous system becomes the central focus, and in breaking free from danger responses, your emotions are given more dominion than your own intellectual guidance system. In fact, your emotions that come from your fight, flee, or freeze reactions become the passageway from going from your sympathetic to parasympathetic processing, from negative and reactive thinking to expanded mental and emotional functioning, and from lowered expectations and living to get by to expanding your mind and emotions and going after your dreams.

From a traditional standpoint, this approach would be seen as irrational because your emotions should not garner this much focus. Also, by going upside-down, your life is not seen from a problem-solving model focusing on external circumstances and small change, but rather more on your internal processes and seeing yourself in a greater context. The goal in this approach is to:

- use your sympathetic nervous system to identify the areas of your life that are viewed as dangerous

- utilize your guided emotions of anger, fear, and indecision to go from the sympathetic to the parasympathetic and unlock your suppressed desires

- use your pleasure sensors in your brain to identify the negative thought patterns that are the source of your sympathetic processing and release them.

In doing this, you are using your body as a guide to help you heal, overcome your internal obstacles, and open the door to the life that you always wanted to live. This approach requires you to trust yourself, to see yourself already as a whole and complete person, and ultimately to train your body and mind to understand that all of the answers you have been looking for your whole life are already within you. This approach takes work, and it requires you to be active and more self-aware in your daily life.

An immediate example of this upside-down approach is the whole process of taking a cold shower. Initially, the mind and body would resist the desire to do so and racing thoughts of "It is too cold!" and "I do not want to do this!" would be front and center. At this point, your mind and body would be thought-focused, being top-down, and the negative filter of thoughts and staying in your comfort zone would be your primary action. However, if you decided to go upside-down, you would need to bypass your mind, address the feelings of danger associated with taking that shower, and allow your sympathetic nervous system to be your guide. Once you turned on that water, your body would react by shouting, "It's cold!" and a shivering of your body would occur, and the negative filter of your mind would dissolve due to your body being in shock. The body would eventually adjust to the cold water, and you would go from the sympathetic to the parasympathetic state. The feeling of danger would eventually subside, and you would go into a proactive response continuing the shower by shampooing your hair, soaping your body and rinsing yourself off. There would be a great relief in the body, knowing that there was no danger and that you could handle the perceived dangerous situation. And as you would step out of the shower and allow the warm towel to touch your body to dry off, the parasympathetic system would fully be present as you would feel warmer, more alert, and in an expanded state.

This transfer from the sympathetic to the parasympathetic state, going from top-down to upside-down and using your nervous system over your mind, is what this approach is. By using this method, you are figuratively taking an internal cold shower every day! This upside-down approach has not only helped Jim, who has been mentioned several times in this chapter, but several clients whom I have had the pleasure of working with. Many clients, after using their own upside-down processing, are now living the life that they always wanted to live. The reason is because the daily internal cold showers that they took shocked their mind and bodies out of their negative thinking and comfort zones. This allowed each person to explore all aspects of who they were and to become experts in their own lives. In becoming your own expert, you take away the stronghold of the sympathetic nervous system when it comes to your emotional world, and you open the door to living your best life.

Let's get to work!

Chapter 2

Casinos and Chocolate Cake

In this chapter, we will be taking a look at depression and anxiety from the point of view of casinos, cell phones, and chocolate cake. And if you are confused, it is okay because depression and anxiety from a nervous system upside-down point of view looks completely different from a traditional top-down perspective. From a top-down point of view, depression and anxiety are about low self-esteem and motivation, while from going upside-down, it is about having too much self-esteem and misdirected ambition. So, yes, from an upside-down perspective, the greater the depression and the anxiety symptoms you have, the more you will need to humble yourself and not let arrogance get in the way of your happiness again. And when it comes to casinos, cell phones, and chocolate cake, it is because the pleasure sensors that fire in your brain can be activated either through pleasure, manipulation, or through emotional pain.

So if you are in great pain from depression and anxiety, just know that it is because of your pleasure sensors in your brain firing and because you are suppressing the best aspects of who you are. This chapter will explore the various viewpoints associated with depression and anxiety, as you become more educated on an upside-down approach.

Depression and Anxiety

In defining depression from a psychological perspective, the universal definition is to have a negative view of the self, the world and your future. Symptoms include:

- persistent sad, anxious, or "empty" mood

- having symptoms for at least two weeks

- feeling depressed most of the day almost every day

- loss of interest in activities that one used to enjoy

- significant weight loss or weight gain

- excessive guilt

- thoughts of suicide.

Depression is a common illness worldwide, with more than 264 million people affected according to the World Health Organization. Depression is different from usual mood fluctuations and short-lived emotional responses to challenges in everyday life. When the symptoms become long-lasting, either with moderate or severe intensity, depression can become a serious health condition. It can cause the affected person to suffer greatly and function poorly at work, at school, and in the family. At its worst, depression can lead to suicide, and it is estimated that close to 800,000 people die due to suicide every year. Suicide is the second leading cause of death in fifteen-to-twenty-nine-year-olds, and the burden of depression and other mental health conditions is on the rise globally.

Depression results from a complex interaction of social, psychological, and biological factors. People who have gone through adverse life events (unemployment, bereavement, psychological trauma) are more likely to develop depression which in turn leads to more stress and dysfunction, worsening the affected person's life situation and depression itself.

In defining anxiety from a traditional standpoint, it is having a helpless view of the self, the world and the future. Symptoms of anxiety include:

- experiencing excessive anxiety and worry

- feeling restless or keyed up

- irritability

- muscle tension

- racing thoughts

- experience of fatigue

- difficulty sleeping.

Experiencing occasional anxiety is a normal part of life. However, people with anxiety disorders frequently have intense, excessive, and persistent worry and fear about everyday situations. Often, anxiety disorders involve repeated episodes of sudden feelings of intense anxiety and fear or terror that reach a peak within minutes, which can lead to either anxiety or panic attacks. These feelings of anxiety and panic interfere with daily activities, are difficult to control, are out of proportion to the actual danger, and can last a long time. Individuals with anxiety may avoid places or situations to prevent these feelings, and often symptoms start during childhood and teen years, extending into adulthood. Examples of anxiety disorders include generalized anxiety disorder, social anxiety disorder (social phobia), specific phobias, and separation anxiety disorder.

Several factors can play a role in depression and anxiety. It can come from environmental factors that are taking place in your life as well as from biochemistry, where certain chemicals in your brain are contributing to one's mood. It can also come from genetics if there is a family history and finally from your own personality and how you cope. Often times when individuals come in for treatment, they are told that their symptoms of depression and anxiety are due to having low self-esteem, having goals that are not reasonable and attainable, and because of past circumstances in life that have shaped their experiences.

Typical treatment of depression and anxiety includes medication treatment from a psychiatrist and psychotherapy services with a clinician where you address the negative thought patterns that are taking place within you. It is also important to note that depression and anxiety go hand in hand. If one is suffering from primary symptoms of depression, a secondary outcome of anxiety will occur because of the overwhelming feelings due to the difficulty of dealing with everyday tasks. Similarly, if someone's primary symptoms are anxiety, a secondary outcome of depression will take place because of the constant use of the fight-or-flight energy which will directly lead to fatigue and low energy.

Redefining Depression and Anxiety

With that, I am going to offer a new way of looking at depression and anxiety from an upside-down approach. My definition of depression and anxiety is simply being stuck in a reptilian nervous system response to everyday quality of life issues, because of the unconscious choice to choose emotional safety over pursuing your dreams and goals. By making this choice, the body experiences a reptilian takeover of your emotional world, which leads to:

- depression because of the negative filter of thinking where life is only seen from a survival point of view

- anxiety because of the helpless belief in outer circumstances, leading to trying to mind-read what other people are thinking, as well as trying to predict the future

- having difficulty making decisions because an immediate and perfect outcome must be guaranteed to be emotionally safe.

That means that if you can remove the sympathetic component out of your emotional world, a great deal of your depression and anxiety symptoms can be alleviated. Depression and anxiety from a nervous system perspective are not about low levels of self-esteem due to being less of a person or having less talent than others, but rather they are caused by the internal dichotomous nature that is taking place within one's emotional world. In fact, most of the clients whom I treated for depression and anxiety are some of the most brilliant and talented people that I have ever met. In treating these incredible individuals, it was never about low self-esteem and drive as much as it was about having high self-esteem with the ambition to never feel pain again. When an individual decides to pursue this goal, which can never be achieved, the symptoms of depression and anxiety are due to the impossibility of the outcome, not because of the person's self-worth. In seeking success in that state, one is not mentally and emotionally available to achieve their desired goals. And in this state, the outcome becomes the same disappointing result over and over again, creating the same cyclical self-fulfilling prophecy and belief of "It is better to stay disappointed than to pursue my dreams at all."

And that is what emotional safety is; it is simply staying in the continuous state of disappointment, so that you can never go from happiness to disappointment ever again. The reason the body reacts this way is that once an impossible goal is set out, everything in life is now perceived as dangerous because any outcome or situation can cause pain. Just like if a gunman had a gun to your head right now, quality of life issues like happiness would be suppressed and thrown out the window at that moment, and the sympathetic nervous system's sole job would be to keep you physically safe at all costs. In fact, happiness in a life-threatening situation would be a deterrent to survival because living requires immediate action. The body would either fight, flee, or freeze in that situation, and your pleasure sensors in your brain would turn on to help you better deal with pain and to stimulate you to try and get out of that situation. Similarly, when a decision is made by an individual to choose emotional safety over pursuing the life that they truly desire because of past painful experiences and not wanting to experience them again, the sympathetic nervous system will then interject itself and bring its same operating system into your emotional world.

The reptilian response will then cause the body to go into emotional safety or being constantly disappointed, with the ultimate goal of focusing on protection over happiness. From an emotional sympathetic standpoint, your dreams are the gunman physically holding a gun to your head twenty-four hours a day, seven days a week. If you can break the unconscious thought-form and consciously become more aware of this state, you can retrain your nervous system to only focus upon physical life-threatening situations and emotionally become more free. In doing so, you would break the perceived dangers of emotional pain, decrease depressive and anxious symptoms and become more open by breaking free from your own mental and emotional prison. Bruce Lee's famous saying about emotional pain is "To find safety, you must enter the heart of danger." Through this approach, you are entering your own emotional heart of danger, but in the end, discovering that there was no real danger at all. That is why from an upside-down standpoint, depression and anxiety can be alleviated by proactively pursuing the internal pains that need to be reprocessed through your nervous system, and ultimately be healed.

Freud, from a psychodynamic point of view, believed that depression and anxiety were due to an individual being overly narcissistic and completely self-absorbed with oneself. From this perspective, depression and anxiety are due to excess levels of self-esteem that lead to grandiose goals. Freud coined this unhealthy coping skill as *idealizing* because an individual is seeking an ambition that cannot exist and is seeking a special and magical way of living that is apart from others. And once an idealized goal like having no pain is sought out, the sympathetic nervous system will remain on, constantly staying in a negative cycle of depression and a helpless cycle of anxiety. It is a completely different paradigm to see an individual who is suffering from depression and anxiety as being too self-absorbed and cocky, but in viewing it this way, you are seeing the painful symptoms as a nervous system issue because of the suppressing of the great talents within an individual. And in treating depression and anxiety for over twenty years, this premise has held up because I rarely saw self-esteem as being the primary cause of my clients' symptoms. In fact, whenever someone with these symptoms would share their stories, they would constantly highlight how talented and skilled they were, and how at the same time, they had to hold back those gifts due to past experiences. And as the emotional layers of the onion became peeled, buried underneath the depression and anxiety were the most confident and self-assured individuals that I have ever seen.

Along with that came a high level of ambition, drive, and a belief that they were truly different from everyone else, and that they could accomplish their idealized goal. I would constantly hear statements like, "There has got to be a different way for me," and, "I know I am special, and there is a special path made just for me." Ultimately, it was having each client admit that those statements at the core were the desire to find a pathway of achieving success without experiencing any emotional pain. From this perspective, the key then for an individual to alleviate suffering from depression and anxiety would be to:

- humble oneself and recognize that you will need to go through the same processes of life as everyone else

- allow all of the suppressed gifts, talents and abilities of the individual to emerge.

In working with these clients, humility was the first bottom level step to get out of that disappointed sympathetic state and to recognize the similarities that they share with all of humanity. This will then lead to the upper processing of an expanded mental and emotional state and a shift from the sympathetic to the parasympathetic nervous system.

Pleasure Sensors in the Brain

Imagine right at this moment that you are eating a delicious piece of chocolate cake. At the moment you put it into your mouth, extreme joy and happiness would come over you as the pleasure sensors in your brain would be firing because of the enjoyment of eating the cake. This is a typical and understandable concept of how the brain uses and fires pleasure sensors when something enjoyable is occurring. However, the pleasure sensors also have a secondary function related to your nervous system. In times of perceived helplessness and desperation, either physical or emotional, pleasure sensors in your brain will fire to help you:

- to fight to overcome that situation

- to flee to get out of the perceived helpless situation

- to freeze by being more accepting of the bad situation.

In each of these scenarios, the pleasure sensors fire in order for you to deal with physical or emotional pain more effectively. From a physical standpoint, if you were involved in a physical altercation with someone, your sympathetic nervous system would take over, and the pleasure sensors would turn on to help you to fight, flee, or freeze in that scenario. More specifically, you would either win the fight, run from the fight, or take an ass-whipping. Either way, the pleasure sensors would be there to help you to cope with the pain.

Similarly, from an emotional standpoint, if you are in a disappointed sympathetic state and an external stimulus comes that can trigger your pain, the sympathetic system would take over, and the pleasure sensors would fire using your fight, flee, and freeze responses through your emotions. In this scenario:

- the fight response emotionally comes in the form of anger

- the flee response emotionally comes in the form of fear

- the freeze response emotionally comes in the form of indecision.

In a physical situation, the fight, flee, and freeze response is based on overcoming external circumstances, and once it is achieved, the sympathetic transfers to the parasympathetic system and the pleasure sensors in the brain turn off. However, from an emotional standpoint, if you use your emotions of anger, fear, and indecision to guide you internally to the source of your pain, you can identify the unhealthy and limiting belief within you, and successfully move on. Just like an emotionally distraught person bypassing their thoughts by taking a cold shower or bungee jumping off of a cliff, you can shift out of the sympathetic system and immediately move towards a parasympathetic state.

When a deep emotion is triggered within you, it is due to the pleasure sensors firing at the same time, because your whole nervous system is assisting you to solve that pain. However, when this occurs, most individuals will try to incorrectly solve this internal problem externally, often by pointing the finger at others, which will then continue the emotional suffering. When I was working with a client who I will name Amy, this was the case. She shared during sessions that she would constantly have difficulty in relation-ships because she always attracted negative people whom she believed held her down in life, because she was so positive and independent. She added that she would often feel used by those individuals around her because they would seek her out for advice, and that she was a very loyal person. It was not until she was redirected during the session to acknowledge that yes, the people around her were negative, but that ulti-mately, she was negative too. And when that was explored with her, at first her anger came directed towards me, but ultimately after processing and taking accountability for her choices, the intensity of her emotions went down because her pleasure sensors went down as well. And it was at that moment, Amy was able to see her own negativity and the fact that she was rather dependent on her life.

Amy acknowledged that when her life became overwhelming, she would try to solve her pain externally by constantly controlling the lives of those around her. And when that did not work, she would just get angrier and angrier pointing the finger at others instead of herself. In fact, once she became accountable for her own actions and looked within, she was able to mentally and emotionally move towards her ultimate goal of being the truly independent person that she desired to be while breaking her loyalty to disappointment in her life. Because if Amy did not, she would have stayed in a sympathetic state with her pleasure sensors remaining on, with the feelings of helplessness and the negative view of her world being reinforced. However, from an upside-down perspective, if you internalize the opportunities to seek out your emotional pain, the body will:

- shift out of anger, fear and indecision

- turn off your sympathetic response by addressing it internally

- turn off the pleasure sensors in your brain by going into parasympathetic processing.

If you try to solve an internal problem externally, the body will react by keeping the sympathetic system and the pleasure sensors on. This will then keep the symptoms of depression and anxiety going, through racing thoughts based on negative beliefs and helpless views. Another example of this is a breakup of a relationship where the person who is broken up with will constantly call the other individual and continue to seek closure. And no matter how many conversations and no matter how many times they meet, the individual continuously seeks out that ex-partner. This is an example of an internal problem seeking to be solved externally. The sympathetic system will act helpless to its environment while the pleasure sensors continue to stay on, and the body will try to externally solve that emotional pain through that person. This continued desire to solve it externally sends the message to the body that this is a desperate situation, and continued self-loathing actions will occur. In truth, the only way for that individual to move on is to be internally guided by their fear and to learn the lesson of "I will have more self-respect for myself right now and in future relationships moving forward." This internal action will turn off the pleasure sensors in the brain, shift from the sympathetic to the parasympathetic, and allow that individual to begin the process of true growth. That is why when individuals who experience a negative event continue to seek an external solution, they will continuously share that negative story to others over and over again. And when they tell their stories for the fourth, fifth, and twentieth time, the passion and vigor of the negative event become stronger and stronger.

In fact, each time the story is told, their eyes will light up, their facial expression and body language will become more expanded, and with every intricate detail of the story being told, a liveliness and almost cynical joy will appear. That is because the pleasure sensors in the brain are fully active along with their sympathetic nervous system due to the belief of being helpless. Pleasure sensors can often be misdirected in this way when they are used to stay in a disappointed state. It is vital for an individual who desires to break free from a negative cycle of thinking to use their pleasure sensors to heal, rather than to prolong and continue to identify with their pain.

Redefining Keeping it Real

The urban definition of "keeping it real" is "not being fake or influenced." The explanation expands, stating that it is also "being true to yourself and to your values, but more importantly, not pretending and being something that you are not." And so, I am going to keep it real with you by stating that you are influenced by your sympathetic nervous system more than you think. Whether it is going to a casino, using your smartphone, driving, watching tv, or even eating potato chips, your sympathetic system is involved. For example, when you go to a casino floor, every aspect of that casino was created through behavioral psychologists to evoke reptilian sympathetic responses in you.

In a natural state, if you brought a hundred-dollar bill and went to the blackjack table and put the money down and lost, your natural reaction would be to put your head down looking at the floor in disappointment, and you would probably decide not to play again. And casino management knows this, which is why when you walk in, they first request that you exchange money for colorful chips, offer free drinks, and get you situated to be more impulsive. And if you look at the design of the casino, at eye level there are bright lights with beautiful displays showing how much money you could possibly win, along with beautiful wait-resses everywhere serving you. Also, there are no windows or clocks, so time cannot be tracked, and the floor always has carpet with unappealing designs. Every aspect of that casino was designed to evoke that reptilian response of desperation in you, by having you seek the external outcome of gambling to achieve your financial dreams.

So, going back to that blackjack table as you bet and lose your hundred dollars' worth of colorful chips, it would feel less painful because you are not seeing your actual money being lost, and if you put your head down due to disappointment, the ugly floor design would cause you to immedi-ately look back up at all of the shiny lights and colorful displays of how much money you could possibly win. And over several conditioned programmed cycles of putting money down, losing, not putting your head down anymore and looking up at all of the displays and lights, the reptilian response of "I do not have enough money" and the external desire to get it would trigger your sympathetic response and the pleasure sensors in your brain. Even the saying so common in Las Vegas, "Well I only lost what I brought, so that was a good trip," is a result of a sympathetic reaction. But that level of intricacy and manipulation is a part of our everyday world as well. Take our smartphones for example. Every aspect of that smartphone was created by using behavioral psychology. All smartphones contain constant push notifications which evoke an immediate reptilian reaction to respond to it, along with extremely fast information cycles that mimic the same speed of our racing thoughts.

Also, if you look at all social media platforms, the design of the reptilian fight, flee, or freeze response is on full display as individuals seek to dominate by being an influencer, act submissively by being a follower, and indecisive internet trolls and keyboard warriors passive-aggressively cyberbullying online. In fact, the phone is identi-fied in the technological world as human consciousness because it tracks every aspect of what the owner likes and dislikes, and all of the impulses each individual has. Your phone is able to account for your level of health, what you do every day, who you are as a person and what purchases you make as a consumer. The primary purpose is to track and maintain a sympathetic structure to each customer so that each new phone that comes out year after year will be bought by you. And in the very near future, Elon Musk was quoted in Forbes (2019) stating that they are working on creating microchips that are to be implanted directly into the brain, so that it can be directly linked with your smartphone. The ultimate goal with these microchips is to use this brain-reading technology to coordinate directly with the pleasure sensors in your brain so that we, the consumers, will stay continuously in the sympathetic state to want to buy more and more products. That is why people cannot live without their phones – because it feels like life or death if they do not have them. And with the increased use of smartphones and social media technology has come the exponential increase in depression and anxiety symptoms. The reason is that, globally, our quality of life has been taken over by our sympathetic world as we substitute our natural parasympathetic thinking with technological consciousness.

Whether it is commercials and ads that seek to send the message that you are not complete unless you buy this car or piece of clothing, to the potato chip that is chemically induced to create a bliss point where it will cause the pleasure sensors in your brain to feel satisfied but wanting more at the same time, it is time to get out of this cyclical loop and truly assess our lives from a different state.

As I am writing this book, we are going through the coronavirus global pandemic which is creating the sympathetic by-product of separation through racial profiling, hoarding water, toilet paper, and hand sanitizers, to sadly the incredible number of deaths due to the handling of this situation. On the news cycle every day, you can see the sympathetic response of the fight, flee, and freeze reactions by our world leaders, and the emotional responses of anger, fear, and indecision from our global community. It is time to wake up. And as everyone is being quarantined and isolated, we all have the opportunity to assess our lives, expand our mental and emotional capacities, and start living in a parasympathetic state of mind. With this invisible virus that can only be seen microscopically, it is incredible how no amount of money or power can stop this pandemic. It is humbling how the only solution to move beyond it requires a shift from the sympathetic to parasympathetic processing through global cooperation.

The current communal acts of staying home, practicing social distancing, supporting frontline workers such as nurses and market staff, and sharing resources and information are just some of the small steps that have already been taken. On all levels of living, whether micro, mezzo, or macro, this pandemic has forced us all to keep it real.

Redefining Success

When it comes to defining success, individuals like Bill Gates, Dwayne Johnson, and Scarlett Johansson come to mind because of their fame, wealth, and the adoration that they receive around the world. And though they are all successful in their own right, I want to offer an even more ambitious definition of success that goes beyond external means. This level of success transcends what you have, what you do, and how many followers you have on social media. In fact, it goes beyond the noise of what you have been told by society, what you have been told by your family and friends, and even beyond your own personal story of why you have not succeeded and are not living the life that you want to live.

This level of success is personal because it comes from being able to come to terms with all aspects of your life, including your greatest pains. In fact, from a parasympathetic standpoint, this level of success means that you have not only escaped the emotional gunman that has plagued your life, but you have completely eliminated their existence. The past pains associated with perceived emotional dangers are now lifted, and you are living in a continuous parasympathetic state. And once you are in this state, you have:

- a clear mind that has significantly reduced racing thoughts

- mental and emotional expansion where you are more open and receptive to your life

- a feeling of genuine peace and safety.

And so, with this premise, I redefine success as being:

The mental, emotional and physical state of no longer living in disappointment by going from the sympathetic to the parasympathetic structure in everyday life and now pursuing your dreams over your pain.

This level of expanded living can be achieved at any moment, and if done through daily practice, can create successive moments where you become more empowered on a continual basis. This level of success is not defined by societal standards but comes through true inner exploration, where you have reached an expanded state by coming to terms with where you have been, where you are, and what you will do in the future. And once you are in this continual parasympathetic state, you have found the greatest wealth and success in the world, which cannot be achieved externally, and that is inner peace.

Chapter 3

Stabilizing Your Nervous System Functioning

When it comes to stabilizing your nervous system and getting out of the state of disappointment, it is important to see depression and anxiety from an upside-down point of view. From this perspective, depressive and anxious symptoms are the product of having too much ambition and too much self-esteem, which is why this impossible goal of no emotional pain was sought out to be achieved in the first place. Individuals with this ambition will seek it out by perfectionistic means through simultaneously striving for excessively high personal standards while providing overly self-critical evaluations. Living in disappointment is the product of being the ultimate overachiever and the by-product of believing that one can achieve the goal of never experiencing pain again, while secondarily achieving their dreams all at the same time. And once this becomes the goal, the experience of no pain completely consumes an individual because of the black and white (life or death) nature of the nervous system, and dreams and life pursuits take a back seat to this "out of the question" goal. And with that inability to reach an impossible goal comes the ongoing symptoms of viewing the world negatively and feeling helpless from the racing mind, because one needs to stay in that state of pain to figure out how not to experience that pain again. It is commendable to pursue this goal because of the effort that is required, and it takes great humility to lower one's ambition from the unattainable goal of never suffering, to stepping down to the goal of living the life that you want to live. It is definitely a less ambitious undertaking, but it is still a virtuous goal to openly pursue happiness and to give yourself permission to allow your gifts and abilities to re-emerge.

To further this process, one will need to understand that stabilizing the nervous system will require one to delineate from the physical world of danger versus the emotional world of danger. More specifically, it is teaching the nervous system that when it comes to one's emotional world, there is no outside danger and that emotions in and of themselves hold no reason for caution whatsoever.

If you are starting the process of getting out of the state of disappointment, then the humility of choosing your dreams and desires over emotional safety is required, which means:

- accepting that good aspects of life come with difficult times

- that pursuing dreams and happiness also comes with emotional pain and challenges

- that the desire to escape pain has not worked and it is emotionally safer pursuing your dreams

- that in pursuing your dreams, your gifts and talents are now leading you instead of your sympathetic processing.

This falls in line with the principle of nature as a beautiful budding rose needing the dirty and sticky mud from the ground for it to grow. In all of existence, this polarity is needed because it allows for a greater expansion and understanding of life.

In psychology, this is known as a *dialectical perspective*, which simply means that multiple truths can exist at one time. And when you start to prioritize pursuing your life goals overstaying in disappointment, various emotions and perspectives will come to you because you are no longer living in a survival state. This is where the parasympathetic state of potential and possibilities opens up.

When living in the sympathetic state of disappointment, the opposite is true, as everything is dichotomous going from one extreme to the other, meaning all or nothing, life or death and black or white. And so in breaking out of the sympathetic state and transitioning to a parasympathetic way of functioning, the choice has to be made to prioritize not only your dreams and pursuit of happiness but also your willingness to pursue the pain that is still held within you. It is through finding your pain that you can have those cold shower moments and truly set yourself free.

Moving forward, you do not even have to know what your goals and dreams are, but you just have to be willing to change your priority by going for it and getting out of disappointment. And as you do this, going upside-down means that instead of seeking answers in your mind, moving forward you will allow your guided emotions to lead you.

10/90 and The Sympathetic Nervous System

Emotional pain that is stored in your nervous system is the result of the process known as "learned helplessness." As stated several times in this book, the nervous system, particularly the sympathetic system, comes in action when something is seen as dangerous because you are helpless to your outside circumstances and you need to fight, flee, or freeze your way out of the situation.

This case is true when you are in real physical danger, but it does not hold true for emotional pain. In fact, you hold the control when it comes to your emotional life, and once you start to exercise this power, you can go towards the process of getting out of the state of disappointment and start living the life that you want to live. When it comes to why the sympathetic system activates in your emotional world and why it goes into this state of disappointment, the reasons come from the following cycle:

- experiencing a very painful emotional event(s)

- viewing the perceived negative

experience(s) in learned helplessness by believing it is due to others and circumstances

- making the decision to never experience that pain again.

And once you are in this state, learned helplessness takes over. Learned helplessness is the belief that 90% of your emotional wellbeing is based on your environment, and 10% is based upon you. This means that the quality of your life and wellbeing is determined by what you do externally and is almost completely dependent upon other people and the circumstances of your life. The behaviors associated with this belief system are being cautious, over-respecting other people, and constantly diminishing yourself in everyday situations. And if you are deeply in the throes of depression and anxiety, you will actively seek a special way to get out of this situation to try to escape the pain. This belief system will then continuously keep the sympathetic system on, and your body will constantly be in a reactive state of living. When this occurs, your body will react by:

- being on high alert seeking an immediate response

- having racing thoughts of negativity and helplessness occurring, leading to greater depression and anxiety

- pleasure sensors in the brain constantly staying on as the body tries to get out of the disappointed state.

From a physiological standpoint, an example of this occurrence is when anxiety symptoms become so high that people will say that it feels like a bee is buzzing in their brain. This is because of the racing thoughts of helplessness continuously occurring, along with high alert responses from your nervous system and the pleasure sensors firing in your brain all at the same time. Another example is when someone is caught up in their depression as they are constantly angry with racing thoughts about all the ways their life is not working, and combined with the nervous system and pleasure sensor responses comes the experience of constant headaches and outbursts. In each case, learned helplessness is maintaining emotional safety by suppressing all of your talents and at the same time leading you towards isolation. That is why depression and anxiety are so painful because the ultimate disappointment of seeking safety is divergently opposed to going in the direction of your dreams.

90/10 and Nervous System Processing

The 90/10 principle is an empowered approach that is the opposite of the 10/90 learned helpless-ness model. The 90/10 principle states that 10% of your emotional response is based on what happens in your external environment, which then triggers the 90% of the emotions that are within you. Through this model, circumstances are not the cause of your emotional pain, but rather they are the stimulus that triggers the stored emotions that are already inside. And once you take this approach, your nervous system will start to stabi-lize because it is no longer seeing your emotional wellbeing as an external desperate situation, but rather an empowered position where you can internally resolve any pains that you have. This approach will also help to reduce the immediate impulses of the nervous system as well as the pleasure sensor responses in the brain.

An example of the 90/10 principle is a client I worked with who suffered from social anxiety and experienced constant anxiety attacks when in social situations. And when he was coming up towards the building to see me, he shared that he waved to a stranger and said, "Hello," and the stranger completely ignored him and went right on his way, not acknowledging him. When he shared what happened, he first had a 10/90 learned helplessness approach as he responded: "I don't know what I did to not have that person say 'Hello' to me and that really hurt my feelings because it took a lot of courage for me to do that." He then expressed how he was having an anxiety attack right at that moment and how he would never socialize again because of the pain. He then went on asking me questions like, "How can I control and get other people to not be mean to me?" and, "How is it possible that people don't have the same reactions I have when other people hate you like that guy?" His complete point of view was that he had very little control of his wellbeing (10%) and that it was almost completely based off of his environment and what others do (90%). His sympathetic nervous system was on full display as he was in flee mode, sharing how he wanted to leave the session.

While he was experiencing shortness of breath and a racing heart, he began sweating profusely, telling me how he was losing control and that this anxiety attack was really bad. We went upside-down by first addressing his nervous system, and I told him, "You can totally lose control right now and have as bad an anxiety attack as you want right now." He looked at me, confused, then paused and from there shared, "I feel like my heart is about to explode, and I might have a heart attack!" I then told him, "I want you to try your hardest to have your heart come out of your chest right now and have a heart attack. I will call 911 if I need to." With the permission to have the symptoms, he began to calm down after six minutes, and he started transitioning from a sympathetic to a parasympathetic state.

As he became calmer, we transitioned into his cognitive processes, shifting him from a 10/90 to a 90/10 point of view. The client and I took the same situation that triggered his anxiety attack, and from a 90/10 perspective, I asked him, "Did you know this person?" He responded "No." The next thing that I asked was, "Is it possible that he may have just been pre-occupied with his own thoughts and possibly did not see you say hi to him?" He replied, "Yes, that is a possibility." I then asked, "Is it possible that he may have been having a bad day, and it had nothing to do with you?" He then responded, "Oh man, I feel bad for him if that is the case." At that moment, I asked him "How do you feel now?" And he replied, "I don't feel nervous at all, and I feel great." The reason was that we stabilized his nervous system processing through internal resources, and as he continued to look within by answering those internal questions, his danger response shut off as well as his pleasure sensors in the brain. He shared at that moment, "This is the feeling and state of mind I have been searching for my whole life." He added, "I don't feel so socially awkward right now, and this is great." We did not explore his self-esteem or self-worth, but simply, we went upside-down. We stabilized his nervous system with the help of his environmental trigger, shut down the pleasure sensors that were activated, and internally addressed the solution. And as he went from a desperate state to an empowered one, he had his cold shower moment. His response was similar to being in physical danger, as he escaped the life-threatening event and then escaped to safety. The only difference was that emotionally there was no danger at all and that ultimately, he was the answer to his own emotional freedom. That was the first lesson for that client in overcoming and releasing his stored pain.

So, from this perspective, this means each day that you live and each circumstance that you are involved in provides you with the opportunity to heal and to grow. From an emotional 90/10 standpoint, nothing in your environment is dangerous enough to stop you from living the quality life that you want to live. In fact, your environment is here to be of service to you every day. From the old 10/90 paradigm of learned helplessness, the nervous system will internalize that you are smaller than the emotional symptoms of pain due to external circumstances, which will then trigger the danger response and the cognitive thought process of "I can't handle this situation." From this new 90/10 paradigm of establishing internal control of your emotional well-being, the nervous system will internalize safety seeing you as bigger than any external circumstance and emotions, and the cognitive response will be "I can handle this because this is coming from within." So when it comes to dealing with difficult emotions, a 10/90 response would be "I am facing emotional pain," while from a 90/10 perspective, the response would be "Emotional pain is facing ME!" It is remembering that you are not your pain, and no matter the intensity of the symptoms, that it is never dangerous. Remember, your emotional pain is facing YOU every day from now on!

Guided Emotions

Your guided emotions are the emotions that come from your nervous system functioning, specifically, your fight, flee, and freeze reactions, and it is used to guide you out of the stored pain that has been the foundation for staying in the disappointment state of depression and anxiety. From the aspect of the nervous system, the goal here is to internally find the source of your pain which will be triggered externally by your environment and when the time comes, to finally release it. Remember from a 90/10 perspective, the environment which includes situations and other people, is nothing but the trigger (10%), to the internal processes that need healing and correcting within yourself (90%). A good analogy is that when you get emotional and begin to point the finger at someone or something, there are three fingers pointing right back at you. And staying with this analogy, the pointed finger represents the trigger (10%), while the three fingers pointing back at you represent the three guided emotions within you (90%). These guided emotions come from your sympathetic nervous system response, and they are:

- anger from the fight response

- fear from the flee response

- indecision from the freeze response.

In a physical situation, the fight, flee, and freeze response is based on overcoming external circumstances, and once it is achieved, the sympathetic transfers to the parasympathetic system and the pleasure sensors in the brain turn off. However, from an emotional standpoint, if you use your emotions of anger, fear and indecision to guide you internally to the source of your pain, you can identify the unhealthy and limiting belief within you, and successfully move on. When the moment occurs where you are met with a circumstance that triggers one of your guided emotions, you can:

- shift out of anger, fear and indecision

- turn off your sympathetic response by addressing it internally

- turn off the pleasure sensors in your brain by going into parasympathetic processing.

It is also important to remember that the stronger the emotion becomes, the greater the pain that is stored within you. In fact, when you have an extremely deep pain that is triggered by your environment, it will feel extremely chaotic and out of control because at that point:

- the external experience shares similarities to your sympathetic pain

- the learned helplessness of that pain is coming out

- the sympathetic nervous system is on high alert while the pleasure sensors in the brain are firing high.

And once this chaotic experience occurs, it feels so out of control and the energy of the emotion is so high that the most common reaction is to solve it through external means. However, if the opportunity to heal goes through the external process of searching, this will then lead to self-sabotaging behaviors. Self-sabotage is simply seeking an external solution to an internal pain. And if you are living this way, your fight, flee, and freeze responses, along with your emotional responses of anger, fear, and indecision will be used externally, while leading you to outcomes that you do not want. Examples of self-sabotage include:

- fighting with those we care about and pushing them away for no good reason

- fleeing and running from great opportunities by choosing the same

typical unsatisfying outcomes from the
past

- freezing by continuously not making the
decisions that require you to be good to
yourself.

Individuals in this state will stay in the same
sympathetic loop and continue to beat themselves up by asking, "Why do I keep making the
same stupid choices over and over again?" And
the reason is that they will use the feelings of
immediacy from the nervous system and the
pleasure sensors in the brain to externally try and
control everything around them. This is where
impulsive and out-of-control actions take place,
which ultimately leads to regret.

To get to this space, it is important to identify and
stop the self-sabotaging behaviors that people
can engage in. Once again, if you are living in a
sympathetic state:

- you are living in a constant state of
disappointment

- you are consistently engaged in self-
sabotaging behaviors

- you are aimlessly seeking internal

answers of your life through external means.

An example of someone engaging in self-sabotaging behaviors is a client whom I will name Priscilla. She was an extremely bright and driven woman who had her own business, and when it came to her professional life, she had a laser focus and knew exactly what she wanted. When it came to relationships, however, it was another story. Priscilla was a strong, assertive, and very independent woman who celebrated her strengths in her professional life but not in her relationships. When she came into counseling, she would describe how she would get extremely depressed when it came to her dating life because she could not find the man that she wanted.

Priscilla was in her forties, and she shared how she had never been in a relationship longer than three months. She stated that when she would get into relationships, she would often get angry because they were not living up to the standards that she wanted in a man, and if she did find someone who came close, she would become very fearful and start acting passive-aggressively trying to be more submissive. Also, when she did find nice guys who treated her well, she would often feel bored with them and cut them loose while chasing men who would not treat her well at all. Priscilla added, "I know nice guys are sweet, but I don't get the fired-up emotions like when I meet more rugged men." She believed that because of her level of success in her professional life that she deserved a man who measured up to her standards.

When I asked her what she was looking for, she responded by sharing that she wanted a man who worked in Wall Street, who was rich and successful, and who had an athlete body with model looks. Priscilla continued on, sharing that he needed to be a manly man who hunted on weekends but who also had a sensitive side and read poetry at night. And in terms of communication, she stated: "My man needs to be a good listener, but also a person that can put me in my place when I get out of line." When Priscilla told me her criteria, I responded by saying, "Wow, that is one impressive man." After that, I followed up with her and responded, "Okay let's say that you found a man exactly like that, but then he shared with you that he wanted a twenty-two-year-old supermodel who graduated at the top of her class, who also cooks and cleans, is basically a super-woman who has a professional career and is a full-time mother and homemaker and still can maintain her looks all at the same time. Can you be that woman?" Priscilla looked dejected, breaking out of her negative filter of thinking and shared, "No, but I am special just as I am."

At that moment, we began to explore her history, and she shared how when she was growing up, her dad had left her family when she was very young. She also added that her mother raised each of her siblings to be independent and that she always was. She added that she had heard stories about her father being a lady's man who would often stay out late and hang around with his friends all night. She stated that she never knew her father, but only heard stories and saw pictures of him. When we explored this more, I asked her, "Was it possible that the fact that your father was not around while you were young may have affected your ideal of what a man should be?" She replied, "Maybe, because what I say I want in a man sounds like a movie character who is not real."

Over the next several sessions, we began exploring her anger, fear, and indecision when it came to her choices in relationships, and those three guided emotions led her out of her disappointed state when it came to her relationships. When she shared her anger about men not living up to her expectations, she needed to show compassion to herself and them because those expectations were imaginary and had no merit. In fact, when she placed those unreasonable external expectations on the men she dated, she was actually placing an unreasonable internal expectation on herself regarding what a woman should be. And her anger that was directed outwardly was really about herself for not measuring up to being that demure and submissive woman she believed she was supposed to be. Also, when it came to her fear of relationships not working out, it was not because she was unworthy, but rather she was suppressing the best part of who she was, which was her assertive and successful side.

In every relationship, she would fearfully try to diminish that part of herself when the relationship progressed, by trying to be the submissive woman that she was not. That is why her anxieties shot high, due to that suppression of her natural assertiveness, not her lack of self-esteem. And by living in this state of disappointment when it came to her view of relationships, she would often make powerless decisions by pushing away the people in her life that would allow her to be the best version of herself, in exchange for chasing her pain and choosing men who were not good to her at all. And as Priscilla used her guided emotions of anger, fear, and indecision while internally processing those emotions, she was able to break free. She transitioned from the sympathetic paradigm of the limited view of relationships to the parasympathetic state of the possibility of being in a relationship where she could truly be her strong and wonderful self. And after her cold shower moment, she began dating quite a bit, meeting men who allowed her to be who she was, and she eventually surpassed the three-month barrier of being in a relationship by eventually getting married.

The moment for her occurred when she met one of the men she dated previously who was stringing her along, and when all of the chaotic feelings from the pleasure sensors and the nervous system fired while he was playing his games with her during their date, she internalized that moment versus chasing him, and processed that this was due to the ideal she constructed because her father was not around. She even shared during the session that she said to herself, "I am chasing my daddy!" And as she fought through those extremely chaotic feelings within her to externally chase this man because of her pleasure sensors and nervous system, she held it together and internalized, "This is about me chasing my fucking daddy!" At that exact moment, she went from learned helplessness to empowerment, from the sympathetic to the parasympathetic, and from a closed negative filter about how she was supposed to be in relationships to an expanded point of view of loving who she was. And right at that moment, she cut it off with that man and all men who did not treat her well after that. Priscilla had her breakthrough moment as if she had just bungee-jumped off a cliff, and she went from feeling extremely scared and helpless to feeling free. Up to that point, Priscilla self-sabotaged herself for over fifteen years, chasing an internal pain through external means, and at the time when she made the transition to internally empower herself, her life changed right at that moment.

It is these seminal moments that are available in your everyday life where the environment triggers your guided emotions, which then goes into the learned helpless feelings stored in your nervous system, which then gives you the opportunity to release from the pain and rewrite the new narrative of your life. Once you transition from a 10/90 to a 90/10 point of view, you are truly living daily as the actor, writer, and editor of your life, all at the same time. And this film set which is your life is guided by your emotions, which then leads to your empowered script about yourself, while at the same time cutting out the learned helpless portions of the story that are not who you are. If you have been living your life like an audition from a 10/90 point of view up to this point, it is time to go upside-down and 90/10, because this story begins and ends in empowerment, as you are the star of this show.

Chapter 4

The Upside-Down Mirror

As we transition into the process of living and implementing an upside-down approach on a daily basis, it is important to take pause and understand what that means. From this point forward, I want you to imagine your life circumstances as a mirror. From a top-down traditional approach, the mirror reflects only what you see in front of you and what is externally happening around you. From this perspective, you are told that the past is not occurring now and that it is important to be rational by being present-focused, to use common sense and use facts to guide you as you deal with your life and your emotions. However, from an upside-down point of view, the mirror provides a different reflection that extends beyond just what you see. In fact, its reflection is quite vast because it reflects your internal mental and emotional state in physical form. From this standpoint, you are either living in your past pains every day, and it is reflected in present time through your environment by the unhealthy choices that you are making, or you are living in the present, making healthy choices focused upon the possibilities of your life and the opportunities that you have in front of you. This can be seen through your relationship dynamics, the professional decisions that you have made, the way you take care of your body, and your overall outlook when it comes to your life. And so every person you meet and every circumstance you are in is a mirror reflecting back to you how you perceive yourself in relation to your life. Also, the distance that you have with the mirror will also dictate how you perceive yourself and your circumstances. The closer you are to the mirror, the less you will see of your environment and the more of yourself you will see. Similarly, the further you are away from the mirror, the smaller your reflection becomes as your environment takes greater focus. Regardless of the distance and space between you and the mirror, the reflection will never lie and will always show you all you need to know about yourself.

The Sympathetic 10/90 Mirror

When it comes to the pain that is stored from your past experiences, the sympathetic nervous system will use that as a guide and try its best to keep you from feeling similar emotional pain in the present and in the future. This then triggers the negative filter of focusing on the worst possible outcomes of your life and being constantly angry due to needing to protect what you have. At the same time, this triggers the helpless feelings within you as your whole mind and body become reactive, living in survival mode over living out your dreams and passions. The mind is in a continuous state of racing thoughts focused upon the difficulties of life, and depression and anxiety symptoms are at the forefront, keeping you in the disappointed state of emotional safety. And in your daily life, any external opportunity that triggers you to internally break out of the sympathetic state will be sabotaged by externally being responded to, keeping your pleasure sensors on as you cyclically seek an external solution to an internal problem.

To shift out of that state, I want you to imagine that you are standing in front of a full-length mirror right now. Imagine that you are about five steps away from the mirror, and you can see yourself in relation to your environment. When you are in a 10/90 state, the first reaction to any emotional pain is to look around your environment and find the reason why you are in distress.

The reflection of the mirror will show you pointing fingers at external things helplessly as you look angry and seek an immediate answer. And in this state, regret keeps taking place because you are in the sympathetic activity of reviewing past decisions based upon external consequences and how you suffered. However, when distress occurs, and you can see the environment as just a trigger for your emotional pain, you can now take several steps towards that mirror and only see your reflection and nothing else. At that moment, you are now internalizing the emotional pain by going 90/10, and you are setting yourself up to release the emotional pain by facing it directly.

You are also taking the danger symptoms and the pleasure sensors out of the sympathetic nervous system by taking away the external point of view. This opens the door for your parasympathetic nervous system to take dominion over your emotional world and opens the door for you to be in a greater mental and emotionally expanded space. When a pain is triggered within you, it is important to change the reflection to more of yourself and less of the environment so that true healing can take place.

The Parasympathetic 90/10 Mirror

The parasympathetic system expands beyond seeing your emotional world as something where survival is needed. In fact, it sees it from a completely expanded space that goes from the possibilities of life to understanding that pain is inevitable. However, it does not view emotions as a life-or-death situation based upon consequences, but rather it sees life as a constant progression moving you towards greater opportunities. In the parasympathetic world, the activity of regret is not needed because it uses perspective instead. When a pain is triggered from your sympathetic system, the parasympathetic structure sees you up close when you heal your pain, as well as seeing you when you take several steps back as you are engaged in your environment. It sees the consequences of unhealthy choices of the past as nothing but another lesson on your own personal journey towards self-growth and expansion.

In this 90/10 mirror, you are carrying your full-length mirror everywhere you go, and you can see yourself in relation to your environment at all times. And when a pain is triggered through an external circumstance, you will walk towards the mirror and internalize the situation to release beyond it, and then take several steps back again to open yourself up to your learned environment once again. You are constantly choosing your dreams and ambitions over living in disappointment, and you are evolving out of the emotional survival responses of blaming, shaming and living in denial. An upside-down day means that you see life going beyond survival and disappointment, and it is extending your mental and emotional space to see the polarity of life that exists. In fact, the greater your perspective becomes, the longer and wider the mirror you carry with you gets. And in that space, the reflection of yourself and your environment continues to grow and become bigger and bigger. Simply put, your external environment is now reflecting your parasympathetic system taking over your emotional world.

Chapter 5

The Upside-Down Day

In the beginning process of implementing this work, your day will be broken down into three parts. The morning time will be specifically used to address your nervous system, which includes your sympathetic and parasympathetic structures, which will then help you to transition into your day as you will use your guided emotions to help you identify areas of your life that need to be addressed, and finally the nighttime, which will be used to reflect and meditate upon the information that was accumulated throughout the entire day.

The goal is to get out of disappointment by eliminating your sympathetic structure in your emotional world and increasing your parasympathetic activity. This daily way of living is going upside-down by choosing your dreams and desires over not trying to experience any emotional pain. The breakdown is as follows.

The morning routine for your nervous system responses of:

- fight

- flee

- freeze

The daytime use of guided emotions of:

- anger to compassion

- fear to freedom

- indecision to empowerment

Nighttime contemplation questions:

- What limiting beliefs were brought to my attention today through practicing compassion? (Anger to Compassion)

- What gifts and talents do I need to cultivate more based on the freedom I exercised today? (Fear to Freedom)

- What are the empowered decisions that I realized based upon choosing empowerment? (Indecision to Empowerment)

- What did I learn about my life today that
  can be used towards pursuing my
  dreams?

So, each day will begin by going upside-down as you prepare your nervous system first, then use your guided emotions during the day, and then utilize your mind processes at night. Most individuals will use the morning time to focus on what they need to do and think about ways of avoiding difficult situations and the possible uncomfortable feelings that may come up, but this approach is different. Instead of telling yourself through repetitive thoughts that you are choosing your dreams and desires over experiencing no emotional pain, you are communicating it through your bodily actions and through the use of your sympathetic nervous system. In fact, your whole day will be about empowering your nervous system, as in the morning you will specifically stabilize and train that there is nothing to fight, flee, or freeze from when it comes to your emotional world.

Secondly, during your day you will then use your guided emotions to identify through environmental triggers your stored pains so that the danger symptoms can be released. And finally, you will transition to the nighttime where you will use your mind for contemplation and meditation by using the lessons of your guided emotions and opening the door for living the life that you want to live. The goal when it comes up to this upside-down approach is to:

- have your parasympathetic structure take over your emotional world, while the sympathetic structure takes a secondary role focusing more on actual physical dangers

- this transition will then allow your goals and dreams to dominate your thought processes over the goal of not experiencing any emotional pain

- this will then lead to you defining the purpose and meaning of your life.

In the previous chapters, you were able to read about clients who had their cold shower moments immediately, but that happened for them over time as they became more used to using an upside-down approach, as well as understanding and incorporating the daily processes that are being outlined for you. The more proficient you become, the greater and faster those breakthroughs for you can happen because you are no longer emotionally inhibited. However, by just following this program daily, you are experiencing the process of a cold shower moment incrementally. From a whole day upside-down perspective, it is being laid out for you to have an emotional cleansing every single day.

When it comes to your daily routine, you will be doing a series of techniques that come from three modalities:

- Neuroscience

- Guided Emotions

- Conscious Choice.

Each of these components will be combined in your morning, day, and night routine as your goal is to restore homeostasis in your overall nervous system. Homeostasis means the balancing of your complete autonomic nervous system where your parasympathetic system activity will increase in your emotional world while the effects of your sympathetic nervous system will be decreased.

This, in turn, will automatically translate to you feeling more clear and present, as well as feeling more mentally and emotionally expanded. It is quite normal as you begin this approach, that you will start to experience excess energy and focus right off the bat. That is a good thing because you are no longer suppressing the stored pain and the suppressed desires that are within your own body. All three of these models tie into the approach and foundation for this work.

Neuroscience

One of the modalities that we will be using is the practice of neuroscience. Neuroscience is the scientific study of the nervous system, and in a broader perspective, it analyzes the relationship between the brain and the broader nervous system functions both through the biological and chemical processes. There is something known as *proprioception*, which basically means the body's capacity to feel where it is in space, which also means that there are periphery means to inform one's feeling state. Neuroscience looks at psychology from an upside-down perspective and recognizes that the use and access of the parasympathetic structure is key to allowing your body to heal and to self-regulate. Studies have found that the use of upside-down processing can help to reverse the stress response that causes:

- an imbalance of the autonomic nervous system with decreased parasympathetic nervous system and increased sympathetic nervous system activity

- an increase in depression and anxiety symptoms due to decreased gaba neurotransmitters that is responsible for sending chemical messages between the nervous system and the brain.

An upside-down approach has been found to produce the reverse response where balance of your whole nervous system takes place with increased parasympathetic nervous system and decreased sympathetic nervous system activity. Simply put, this practice helps your parasympathetic structure to be the primary source of your emotional functioning. This also leads to an increase in the activity of the GABA system through stimulation of the vagus nerve, which is the main peripheral pathway of the parasympathetic nervous system. GABA neurotransmitters are important because when activated through your parasympathetic structure, the brain reduces overstimulation and in turn, reduces the symptoms of depression and anxiety within an individual. This is where the concept of the third eye comes from in yogic practice or the pineal gland. The pineal gland is a small pinecone-shaped gland that lies deep inside the center of the brain in the epithalamus. It is a part of the endocrine system and helps to regulate melatonin, which is a chemical produced in the brain that helps the body to sleep at night. The pineal gland governs the production of hormones as well as the maintenance of the circadian rhythm, which is essential for the sleep cycle. The role of this tiny gland has only recently begun to be understood, and scientists are still studying it to try and completely understand its role and function. What is known is that nervous system processing and activation of the parasympathetic structure helps in activating the pineal gland, and this activation has been identified in a spiritual context from yogic practice to spiritual psychology.

It has long been associated with the idea of the third eye, which is a spiritual symbol of all-knowing according to yoga philosophy, and it is often perceived as a gateway for the soul's liberation. The idea of the third eye has also floated around science circles previously, as some believe the pineal gland is a leftover in the human brain of an actual physical third eye, which we eventually will evolve out of. In addition to the physiological role the pineal gland plays in the body, it is also commonly associated with spiritual thought and mystical experiences. Ancient sages and mystics believed this area of the body to be the space for ascension and enlightenment through the mind-body connection. It is perceived as a bridge between our inner and outer worlds, as well as to a connection to something beyond what we know to exist, often leading to higher states of consciousness.

Outside the realm of science, the pineal gland or the third eye is located between the center of your eyebrows, back deep in your brain. Many ancient yogis believe that when you strengthen and activate the third eye, you will awaken your own inner intuition and wisdom, leading you to the path of self-realization. Symbolically, the third eye represents union on the path to cosmic consciousness, divine wisdom, inner knowing, and intuition. This is the place where the ego is left behind, and the concept of duality begins to unwind in order to embrace unity and the concept of oneness.

That is why the activation and the increased activity of the parasympathetic nervous system are so vital, because the greater the activity of the parasympathetic system within you, the greater the activity of your pineal gland. Many yogic practices, including quiet asana, slow breathing, meditation, and guided imagery, all increase the activation of the parasympathetic nervous system and lead to mental relaxation through the activation of the pineal gland. However, in order to reach balance between the two nervous system structures, we will be incorporating both nervous system structures by tapping into the danger responses of the sympathetic system directly, then creating an escape route, which will automatically open the door to increased parasympathetic activity. This will be a meditative and yet intentionally produced danger response simulation and escape, which will naturally allow for your parasympathetic activity to increase and in turn, activate the pineal gland. Instead of going top-down and trying to use our thoughts to stimulate our feeling responses, we will be using our periphery resources starting in the nervous system, going through the vagus nerve and upwards into the brain, creating greater neuroplasticity.

Through daily practice, this will restore the homeostasis of the whole nervous system structure and naturally will allow for greater mindfulness and presence by going upside-down.

Moving upwards to our feelings and thinking through this process all leads to greater neuro-plasticity in the brain. The modern understanding of the brain is that rather than being a static structure, this organ is constantly remodeling itself, which is what neuroplasticity is. The repeated thoughts and actions by going upside-down can rewire your brain, and the more you engage in expansive thinking, the stronger those new neural networks become. And with new neural networks becoming stronger every day, the process will lead to the altering and the diminishing of long-standing dysfunctional behaviors that are associated with depression and anxiety. We will be using a mixture of upside-down techniques to restore the overall homeostasis of your nervous system.

Guided Emotions

Another modality that we will be using is the process of *guided emotions*. Guided emotions came from existential psychology and were developed to encompass the whole mental and emotional spectrum that involves being a human being. Their roots go back to the existential philosophers of the 20th century recognizing that humans are conscious and aware of their own mortality, which means we all have the possibility and responsibility of deciding in each moment what to be and how to live. Existential psychology goes beyond positive psychology because it emphasizes finding meaning in life over promoting self-esteem. An example of this approach is Viktor Frankl, who developed this form of psychotherapy after surviving the Nazi concentration camps during the 1940s. After his experience in those camps, he developed a theory that was based upon his own search for meaning and to come to terms with his own suffering and pain. When Frankl and his family were deported to a Nazi concentration camp, he spent time in four camps over a three-year period, and he was the only member of his family to survive. When he returned to his native home of Vienna, he published several books based upon his recordings and observations during his time in the concentration camps. His book, *Man's Search for Meaning*, in which he wrote about his experiences and his theoretical approach to life has been published all over the world.

Guided emotions are not about trying to contain your emotions and trying to act in a forced restricted way, but rather they are opening the peripheral channels of your being and being available to the true essence and meaning of life.

By going upside-down through using guided emotions, your emotions are not seen as irrational and as something that must be contained, but rather as a guide and signpost to healing and greater self-awareness. From this existential point of view, it is trusting in the natural essence of who you really are as a person and believes:

- that each individual is deep down inherently good and has talents and abilities within them

- that everyday life provides the opportunity to strengthen one's internal resources and strengthen their inner core

- that life offers purpose and meaning, but it is up to you to experience fulfillment and happiness.

Frankl, when he was in the concentration camps, was surrounded by nothing but violence, imprisonment, and death. There was nothing but destitution as he was daily witnessing individuals being killed, as well as many others committing suicide around him. When he discussed how he witnessed first-hand the murdering of his wife by Nazi soldiers, he went from extreme hopelessness and viewing life as completely meaningless, but miraculously switched to a place of finding meaning and purpose at the same time. He mentioned that he was aware of the life-or-death nature of his own existence because of the reality of the situation, but that internally, he explored his expanded nature within him. He was constantly vacillating between his sympathetic survival state and his parasympathetic structure that was seeking a higher purpose for his life.

Frankl believed that if he could survive, he could make a difference in the world and come to terms with this experience of his life. He mentioned having this similar process when he looked at a dead rotting fish on the ground, as he went from looking at it from the point that it was nothing but a carcass and that it reflected the sheer hopelessness of his current situation, to shifting to seeing the beauty in that fish and finding meaning in the fact that it nourished someone to help keep them alive.

This level of mental and emotional expansion is available to us all, and regardless of the circumstances you are in, you have the power to come to terms with where you are in life and find the meaning behind it and move on towards a life of possibility. Guided emotions use six basic assumptions which are:

1. We are all spirit, body and mind.

The belief here is that all human beings consist of all three but that it is the spirit which is the essence of who we really are. This existential approach believes in the polarity that exists between the finite existence of the body and mind versus the infinite soul.

2. All circumstances in life have meaning.

Using guided emotions means believing that every situation in life, including the miserable ones, all hold a higher order for you to strengthen your inner core and to enhance the spirit that is within you. You are to use your internal resources, allowing you the opportunity for greater self-discovery to happen.

3. All individuals seek meaning, but it cannot be achieved through avoiding pain.

The use of guided emotions means coming to terms with your own life and understanding the meaning behind every aspect of your existence. What that means is that you are not only to seek out happiness, but that also means accepting and enduring suffering because there is great meaning in it as well. In taking this approach, guided emotions believes the goal of meaning supersedes seeking happiness or avoiding pain.

4. Every individual must exercise their right to choose meaning.

This approach believes that every circumstance allows for you to find meaning, and if you look within yourself, you can see the purpose behind it. It is through the exploration of the outside world while at the same time internally processing it, that allows for growth and meaning to occur. In finding meaning, you are mentally and emotionally expanding yourself by increasing the activity of your parasympathetic system in your emotional world.

5. There is meaning in the moment.

Guided emotions honor the belief that right at the moment an event emotionally triggers you (90/10), it is up to you to internally understand what this circumstance means to you. When Frankl was in the concentration camps, he had to address the reality of being in an internment camp and his sympathetic reactions, and at the same time internalize the greater purpose for himself beyond it which was his parasympathetic processing. Similarly, this holds true in your daily life as you will need to address the dual components of your nervous system which includes your sympathetic and parasympathetic structures in your everyday world. Each moment holds meaning because when you are choosing your dreams over disappointment, the desire to live out your parasympathetic desires supersedes your desire to act in emotional survival, and each moment you live leads you to greater purpose and expansion in your life.

6. All individuals are unique.

This approach believes that every individual, including you, is a unique expression that came from a divine source of life and that it is up to each of us to express our individualized gifts, talents, and abilities.

One of the techniques that we will be using throughout your day will be a "paradoxical intention." By definition, an intention is to act in a purposeful and a deliberate way, and a paradox by definition is to have an absurdly or contradictory statement when examined to be true. So, when you put this together, this approach means to intentionally and purposefully act in an absurdly contradictory way because it will turn out to be right. An example of this type of paradox can be statements like, "Less is more," or "Truth is honey which is really bitter," and "The less you care about what people think about you, the more they will like you." When it comes to any anxiety or depressive symptoms you may have, you will be intentional in seeking to enhance the symptoms, because in doing so, paradoxically, you will take the danger symptoms associated with the sympathetic nervous system away.

For anxiety and the sympathetic response of learned helplessness, you can set up "worry times" throughout the day and give yourself permission to be as anxious as you want for five minutes at a time. In doing so, you are purposefully regulating the whole nervous system and opening up your parasympathetic response.

Similarly, for depression and the racing negative thoughts from the disappointed sympathetic state, you can set up "angry times" throughout the day and give yourself permission to be as negative as you want at five-minute intervals. These paradoxical approaches will allow you to address these symptoms from an upside-down approach and open the door for proprioception, meaning greater body awareness as well as mental and emotional expansion.

Conscious Choice

Conscious choice uses a reality approach with the focus on addressing an individual's choice and their own personal ability to solve whatever is going wrong in their life. The focus of the model is present-oriented, and the goal is to help create a better future by focusing on the here and now. Choice theory is at the core of this approach, and the purpose is attempting to choose expansion and growth over getting by and trying to remain the same. Being conscious means that from a 90/10 perspective, an individual can look at the relationships in their life, and through awareness identify the limited belief systems and self-sabotaging behaviors that are at the root of one's unhappiness.

Conscious choice sees relationships as a reflective mirror of one's underlying problems because the relationships mirror everything that you need to know about yourself. In anyone's unsatisfying relationships, this will dictate the causes of psychological problems, and conversely, all psychological problems lead to unsatisfying relationships. Therefore, for an individual to be successful, a person must examine their most important relationships and learn the lessons that they have to offer.

The focus of conscious choice is to break things down into step-by-step methods that can make the solutions simpler. The process involves being able to analyze the situation and figure out from the situation what can be changed. From there, it is a matter of having a plan and making sure that the plan is properly executed. It is a very systematic approach that promotes personal accountability and empowers the individual to see that they alone are the solution.

Conscious choice acknowledges, accepts, and takes responsibility for the positive and negative consequences of one's own actions and because of the ability to always make a choice, an individual must also accept the outcomes of their own lives. In understanding this construct, conscious choice focuses on these tenets:

Control – establishing and acceptance of choosing a 90/10 perspective when lead by your guided emotions.

An individual has a conscious choice of expanding beyond a survival response by choosing:

Compassion (from anger)

Freedom (from fear)

negative thoughts and fearful outcomes of what could happen. This leads to the paradoxical outcome of increased anxiety and depressive symptoms because the individual is trying to exert external control over an internal problem. Understanding this dynamic helps to understand the 10/90 Learned Helpless paradigm of GUSR below:

- **G = Guided Emotions** are externalized by blaming the situation

- **U = Unconscious choice** is made by externalizing the situation, and the stored pain within your nervous system is triggered

- **S = Self-sabotage** through learned helpless behaviors take place as your pleasure sensors are turned on

- **R = Reinforced** experiencing of the event promotes anxiety and depression through constant racing thoughts.

This leads to a continuous cycle where your sympathetic system is increased in your emotional world, while your parasympathetic system is decreased. This, in turn, keeps your body in the continuous state of disappointment and living in emotional safety, while your goals and dreams are suppressed and pushed down in the form of resentment and anxiety attacks. Once an individual is able to recognize and break the cycle of depression and anxiety, the next stage then becomes focusing on what the individual wants out of their life. When the guided emotions are internalized, and a 90/10 processing occurs, they can be used to help you identify your goals and dreams. At that point, you can ask yourself meaningful questions from your guided emotions throughout your day to lead you to where you want to go.

In closing, these three theoretical approaches are the foundation for your upside-down day. The day begins by starting from the activation and stimulation of both your nervous system struc-tures which sets the tone for choosing your dreams over not living in disappointment, as we increase the activity of your parasympathetic nervous system. This, in turn, shoots GABA neurotransmitters upwards through your vagus nerve, which directly activates your pineal gland. Similarly, with the use of guided emotions during the day, you are going beyond the mind by tricking it through purposeful and intentional processes that go in line with the dual and para-doxical nature of the nervous system and allows for healing and growth to emerge. And lastly, conscious choice fits in because it seeks for you to be actively engaged in finding the answers of your life through your environment, and especially through your relationships. All three of these models tie in together and create an eclecticism that fits the whole upside-down approach.

Chapter 6

Upside-Down Self-Esteem

Developing self-esteem from an upside-down approach is quite different from approaching it from a top-down perspective. From an upside-down view, self-esteem is not determined by how you think and feel about yourself, but it is directly correlated with the ambition that you have about life. Ambition in this context does not mean trying to be the best or to be number one, but it simply means the desire to expand your mental and emotional capabilities to the point that you experience all aspects of who you are. In this state of ambition, you are able to see beyond consequences and survival because you have expanded your mental and emotional capacity to see the spectrum of all of your emotional processes. From a biological lens, this means the polarity that exists within your own nervous system from the sympathetic to the parasympathetic, and from a life context, this polarity includes the finite nature of your body to the infinite nature of your soul. And it is through this expansion that true strength and growth occur because it transcends the ego's association with the sympathetic nervous system.

Oftentimes from a top-down view, individuals are not willing to step outside of their own comfort zones because of the fear of losing self-esteem and how they view themselves. This then triggers the survival instincts of the sympathetic nervous system, only seeing outcomes based upon consequences and black or white thinking. This progresses to the top-down approach of trying to establish greater mental control by focusing completely on being rational so that your emotions will never get out of hand. In order to do that, this requires a person to remain in an emotionally disappointed state, keeping the sympathetic structure involved in your emotional world, because that is when the mind can estab-lish greater control of one's emotions. Externally, this includes making reasonable goals for oneself, and if and when a situation takes place where one's emotions cannot be contained by rationalizing, all hell breaks loose as the mind loses control, because the emotional guidance system has taken over.

Individuals at this point will then become even more determined to establish greater control through their minds, which then leads to neurotic thinking and pointing the blame to external circumstances like people, places, and situations. The whole purpose is to forcefully prevent any emotions from dominating the mind. This top-down approach's primary goal is to protect your self-worth at all times and to do that, your strong emotions are seen as the enemy.

When emotions become so strong that they go outside of your ability to rationalize, you will say to yourself statements like, "You are acting out of control right now," and "Get yourself together, as you are losing it!" However, from an upside-down approach, self-esteem simply equates to self-preservation. From this perspective, if your physical life is truly not in danger, self-esteem or self-preservation is a wasted activity. In truth, through an upside-down perspective, these emotions that transcend your rationale are not a threat at all but are actually your guide to greater perspective and true emotional freedom.

Timmy Top-Down

I had a client who came in for counseling services seeking help regarding his self-esteem and his ability to perform as a fighter. The client was doing local circuits for boxing tournaments around his area, and he had lost his last five fights. Up to that point, he was undefeated, and he shared, "I thought that I was invincible." He described himself as an aggressive fighter who would take two shots to return one punch back to his opponent. He always moved forward, and he would dominate the will of the other fighter.

When he experienced his first loss, he shared that the other boxer was able to take his punches, which did not happen in his past fights, and that his psychological games of using intimidation did not work. Also, as the other opponent would take his shots he would also fire back punches, which he was not used to experiencing. He shared that at that moment he, the bully, was being bullied, and he began experiencing fear that he never felt before. He also shared that it had really kicked in for him how dangerous this sport really was.

When meeting with me, he discussed how he was working with a sports psychologist before coming to see me who had tried to get him back to his old ways of thinking and becoming that invincible fighter once again. He stated that they worked on using positive self-talk and positive affirmations, as well as having him remember how he used to be in the bouts that he was winning through visualization. Timmy was given the same explanation of how his thoughts create his feelings, which then leads to positive action. However, as the losses kept piling up, he shared that he felt like he was just lying to himself and that the affirmations would just feel fake and forced instead of making him feel better. Also, when he used visualization, he shared that his emotions of fear and regret would just dominate his ability to see himself invincible again. Even when he would watch old videos of himself, he stated that he did not even recognize that person anymore.

When he described what he was seeking from the counseling services, he repeated the same top-down goal as previously, which was, "I want to go back to the old me who felt like he could never be beaten and who had all of the confidence in the world. I would walk through fire, and I was not afraid of taking punches, and the thought of losing was never on my mind." The client added "When I lost, it broke my identity of being invincible and when I perform now, I am always afraid of losing. I even lost to guys that I know I am more skilled than, but my mind is in such a lost space right now." He shared that during his first loss and the several losses after, his body would freeze, feeling like it could not move, and he would just want to run away and not be in the ring. He added, "No matter how hard I tried to talk myself out of it, I could not shake the feeling of being no good and inferior in there when I box now. I felt like my feelings let me down." I let him know that he was successful in being Timmy Top-down using traditional methods which aided in his undefeated record, but when his rationales could no longer contain his stronger emotions that emerged, they took him over because his emotional guidance system wanted him to become even more than just an undefeated fighter. I also let him know that even though it looked like from the top-down that his nervous system and feelings were letting him down, it was actually opening the door for him to become an even greater version of himself.

Billy Upside-Down

When I reviewed with Timmy his previous attempts using a traditional method of treatment, I quickly went over how the upside-down approach would be different. I let him know that instead of focusing on his thoughts incessantly to control his feelings, that we were going to let his feelings go free without any control. This meant that instead of using his mind to feel good about himself, we were going to work on expanding and honoring all of his emotions so that he could be guided and lead through them. This meant for him to immediately face emotions that countered the limited paradigm of being an invincible fighter. We started with his nervous system by stabilizing the dangers associated with him boxing, as well as his danger feelings associated with losing and not being invincible. From there, we used his guided emotions of fear, anger, and indecision to expand his mental and emotional capabilities and lastly, we expanded his sympathetic, consequence-based thinking from wins and losses to a parasympathetic goal of becoming the best fighter that he could be.

As we reversed his treatment plan from top-down to upside-down, Timmy Top-down became Billy Upside-down. And what that meant was that he was evolving beyond who he used to be and was opening himself up to being and experiencing aspects of himself that he was previously suppressing. Instead of trying to take the danger sensations and the emotions away from him, we used them as his guide to discover what was seeking to emerge from him. I let him know immediately that he needed to understand two things before we started, which were:

1. You cannot go back to your old self as a boxer because you are not that person anymore.

2. The strong emotions that cannot be controlled by your mind will lead you to your answers.

When any athletes make the statement of "I am going to go back to the old me," I know that this is the kiss of death to their career. This means that they have run out of all mental options when it comes to dealing with their emotional guidance system taking over and a great demise is to take place. Just like a person cannot go back to being who they were ten years ago, no matter how hard they try, no person cannot stop the progression and evolution of life. And for Billy, it was a matter of using his past to expand his capacities now and in the future.

The treatment that was laid out for Billy is the same approach that will be explained in the following chapters for you. His treatment plan was broken down into parts, starting with his morning treatment using yoga to stabilize his danger symptoms and his overall nervous system. This then led to the daytime where he used his guided emotions when he trained so that he could see the areas where he needed to grow. And then at night, he used contemplation to reflect upon his whole day, using his day's experience as a guide.

Through this process, Billy was able to expand his capabilities as a boxer because he was no longer a one-dimensional fighter who was just offensive-minded. By honoring all of his emotions, he began using more defense in his fights as well as expanding his mental and emotional capacities during his boxing matches. After he embraced his emotions and allowed his emotional guidance system to take over, he excelled again in fighting. His boxing abilities combined his aggressive fighting style with elusive defense as well as being more tactical in the ring. Even the freezing symptoms he experienced in his fights were used to help him understand that fighting wasn't everything for him.

By embracing the danger symptoms of fighting and the fear of not being invincible, it opened the door for him to explore other career paths which eventually lead to him seeking his degree in graphic design. His expanded interests and perspective allowed Billy to see boxing in a parasympathetic viewpoint as one part of his life versus being his whole world.

From an upside-down approach, his emotional guidance system took over and went beyond his rationales. Billy, by going upside-down transitioned from his sympathetic thinking of winning is the only option, to a parasympathetic processing of expanded capabilities and winning in life. As his life progressed and grew to a life outside of boxing, internally Billy Upside-down knocked out his inner Timmy Top-down for good.

Chapter 7

The 30-Minute Morning Routine

One of the things that I want to preface here is that you do not have to be a yoga expert to do any of these exercises that are to be explained. I am no expert by any means, and the sequence of movements was specifically chosen to communicate to our body that we are choosing our dreams and goals over the goal of not feeling any emotional pain. In fact, the whole point of this sequence is to help balance and restore homeostasis in your nervous system functioning and to promote better mental and emotional well-being. The whole routine will take about thirty minutes, which is to be done in the morning, and the goal of which is to:

- promote homeostasis between your sympathetic and your parasympathetic nervous system

- take the danger symptoms out of any emotions that you are trying to avoid

- mentally go from consequence-based thinking to contemplative expansive thinking.

The yoga that we will be doing is known as Paradoxical Intention Yoga. The reason that it is called this is that we will be intentionally contradictory and direct by not using our minds first for better mental health, but instead, we will be going upside-down by starting with our nervous systems. We will also be intentional in seeking out the danger symptoms that we feel inside of us and openly embracing the negative thought-cycles of depression and the racing thoughts of fear. In this paradoxical approach, by embracing the danger, we will feel more open and safe, and the possibilities of your lives open up through our parasympathetic systems.

From an upside-down standpoint, you are taking the fight, flee, and freeze reaction out of your emotional world by communicating directly with it every day first thing in the morning. In fact, the more you engage your nervous system, the danger responses associated with past memories will dissipate because the tensions stored within the nervous system will be released. Your bodily actions of intense breath-work, sympathetic body movements, and parasympathetic body posturing will all be used to stabilize your fight, flee, and freeze reactions, and ultimately separate any associations it has with emotional pain and thoughts. Through the use of this morning routine, you will:

- engage each sympathetic reaction (fight, flee, freeze)

- create a victory, escape and hide route to turn off the danger responses associated with them

- increase the parasympathetic activity in your emotional world by decreasing the sympathetic activity all at the same time.

In fact, just from this work alone in the morning, a greater focus and clarity will automatically emerge because you are strengthening and utilizing your sympathetic structure in a way that it can understand. The yoga will be broken down into three parts.

Sympathetic Triad Yoga, addressing the immediate action response, the pleasure sensors and the racing thoughts:

- Paradoxical freedom "worry time" meditation for two minutes

- Prayer pose and breath of fire for 120 breaths into triumph pose, deep breathing for five breaths

- Balance/imbalance breathing 20x into receiving prayer pose for five deep breaths

- Cat/Cow pose 20x into the sky-reaching pose for five deep breaths.

Parasympathetic Triad Yoga, which will induce the calming response, the activation of your intuition and creating presence:

- Paradoxical compassion "negative time" meditation for two minutes

- Bridge pose for five deep breaths

- Upward facing dog for five deep breaths

- Downward facing dog for five deep breaths.

Homeostasis Yoga, where we will go from the sympathetic to the parasympathetic in helping to engage our survival responses and calming responses directly:

- Breath of fire with Seiken punches, five sets of ten, into hero pose for five deep breaths

- Breath of fire with tuck pose for 120 breaths into upward facing dog and child pose for five deep breaths

- Breath of fire with muscle tension relaxation into corpse pose for two minutes

- Two "Ohm" chants through deep breathing and closing meditation.

The whole sequence will help you to open up to being more body-conscious and more attuned with the guided emotions that come directly from your nervous system. After completing the sequence, it is okay if you feel a burst of energy and a separation between yourself and your mind. This will be the beginning of proprioception as you experience a periphery way of channelling your emotions. One client who performed this shared that he felt a numbness from his mind and at the same time, a pulsing feeling in the center between his eyebrows where the pineal gland is located. In performing this every morning, you are preparing yourself to seek meaning in life over trying to rationalize your emotions. In fact, you will become so intimate with the danger feelings associated with the sympathetic structure, that the danger feelings themselves will feel weaker and less scary over time, which will mean you can feel all emotions in a more natural state. This works in stark contrast with engaging in forced positivity through your mind, which can lead to denial, increased anxiety, and overstimulation of your danger symptoms with your sympathetic nervous system. So, through this method, you are genuinely and naturally becoming more mentally and emotionally available by going to the heart of your emotional pain and being okay with it.

Your body is learning and processing how brave and courageous you actually are. In fact, through your upside-down body structure, you are bravely surrendering and letting go of all limitations that you have stored within yourself, and you are allowing yourself to naturally be who you are. Below is the breakdown of the thirty-minute sequence:

Sympathetic Triad Yoga

Paradoxical freedom "worry time" meditation for two minutes

1. Sit on the floor doing the easy pose, also known as *Sukhasana*, which is a basic seated yoga posture. Simply cross your legs and sit comfortably, sitting up with your back straight while not being rigid.

2. From there, exercise your freedom and intentionally allow yourself to worry as much as you want for two minutes. You can ask yourself the question, *"Is there anything that I want to run from in my emotional world?"* From this point, allow your nervous system and your emotions to run free. If there is resistance in doing so, along with greater fear, this is a great opportunity for you to break the danger symptoms associated with fear right off of the bat.

3. Remember to be intentional with the anxiety symptoms, because they need intentional space where the danger is taken out, and a space to release the tension associated with the feelings.

4. After two minutes, give yourself permission to run to your independent space of emotional

safety. Feel the emotions through your nervous system.

5. Trust yourself and let yourself go for two minutes.

Easy pose and breath of fire for 120 breaths into prayer pose, deep breathing for five breaths

1. Keep the easy pose position.

2. From there, just like a dog panting out of his mouth, do the same with your breathing, in and out of your nose, for 120 rapid breaths.

3. After you complete that, hold your hands near your chest in prayer and perform five deep breaths.

Balance/Imbalance breathing 20x into receiving prayer pose five deep breaths

1. While sitting in easy pose, exhale while extending your arms forward like you are pushing something away with open hands, and then when you breathe in, act like you are gathering something right in to your chest. Imagine that you are pushing something away that you want to let go of while exhaling, while bringing all that you want to yourself as you breathe in, bringing your hands to your chest.

2. After completing twenty breaths, hold your hands upwards, keeping them close to your chest, pointing your head upwards while deep breathing for five breaths.

Cat/Cow pose 20x into the sky-reaching pose for five deep breaths

1. Start on your hands and knees with your wrists directly under your shoulders, and your knees directly under your hips. Point your fingertips to the top of your mat and place your shins and knees hip-width apart. Center your head in a neutral position and soften your gaze downward.

2. Begin by moving into cow pose by inhaling as you drop your belly towards the mat. Lift your chin and chest and gaze up toward the ceiling. Broaden across your shoulder blades and draw your shoulders away from your ears.

3. Next, move into cat pose as you exhale, drawing your belly to your spine and round your back towards the ceiling. The pose should look

like a cat stretching its back. Release the crown of your head toward the floor, but don't force your chin to your chest.

4. Inhale, coming back into cow pose, and then exhale as you return to cat pose.

5. You are going to do this movement twenty times in succession.

6. After completing, you will go into sky-reaching pose where you will put both hands up in the air as you stretch your spine and push your head and neck upwards and do deep breathing for five breaths.

Parasympathetic Triad Yoga

Paradoxical compassion "negative time" meditation for two minutes

1. Sit on the floor in easy pose, as previously explained.

2. While sitting in easy pose, purposefully and intentionally – in a compassionate way – allow yourself permission to feel as negative as you want for two minutes. You can ask yourself the question, *"Is there anything in my emotional world that I feel like I need to protect or defend?"*

3. If there is resistance in doing so, along with greater negativity, this is a great opportunity for you to break the danger symptoms associated with the negative cycle right off of the bat.

4. Remember to be intentional with the depressive symptoms, because they need intentional space where the danger is taken out, and a space to release the tension associated with the feelings.

5. After two minutes, allow yourself permission to break out of protecting your feelings to allowing yourself to be happy. Whatever emerges through

your nervous system and emotions, allow it to take place.

6. Trust yourself and let yourself go for two minutes.

Bridge pose for five deep breaths

1. Begin on your back with the knees bent and the feet planted beneath the knees.

2. Place the feet hip-distance apart and parallel, with the knees and your hips equal distance apart.

3. Notice the natural curve of the neck which is the space between the cervical spine and the floor. Maintaining this natural curve of the neck is crucial because the pose often gets lost when the shoulders are dragged down as they are tucked under. To correct this tendency, shrug the shoulders slightly closer to the ears and observe how this softens the trapezius muscles at the base of the neck and emphasizes the cervical curve.

4. Pressing down with the feet, lift the hips without letting the knees spreading apart.

5. Interlace the fingers beneath the back, then carefully roll the outer shoulders and upper arms

under without pulling the shoulders away from the ears. Pressing down with the shoulders, inflate the upper body lifting the shoulder blades into the chest.

6. Once in the pose, spin the inner thighs down while directing the buttocks towards the backs of the knees. Without lifting the feet, isometrically slide the heels towards the hands to engage the hamstrings and lift the hips as much as you can.

7. Use exhales to press down with the feet and shoulders; use inhales to lift the hips and chest.

8. Do five cycles of going up on the inhale and down on the exhale using deep breaths, holding your breath for ten seconds and then releasing.

Upward facing dog for five deep breaths

1. Lie on your stomach on the floor, stretch your legs back, with the tops of your feet on the floor. Then bend your elbows and spread your palms on the floor beside your waist so that your forearms are relatively perpendicular to the floor.

2. Inhale and press your inner hands firmly into the floor and slightly back, as if you were trying to push yourself forward along the floor. Then straighten your arms and at the same time lift your torso up and your legs a few inches off the floor on an inhalation.

3. Narrow the hip points while firming the buttocks but not squeezing. Firm the shoulder blades against the back and puff the side ribs

forward. Lift through the top of the sternum and look straight ahead or tip the head back slightly.

4. Hold this position while inhaling and holding your breath for ten seconds, and then exhaling as you release on the way down.

Downward facing dog for five deep breaths

1. Come onto the floor on your hands and knees while setting your knees directly below your hips, and your hands slightly forward of your shoulders. Spread your palms, index fingers parallel or slightly turned out, and turn your toes under.

2. Exhale and lift your knees away from the floor. At first, keep the knees slightly bent and the heels lifted away from the floor. Lengthen your tailbone away from the back of your pelvis. With this resistance, lift the sitting bones toward the ceiling, and from your inner ankles draw the inner legs up into the groins.

3. Then with an exhalation, push your top thighs back and stretch your heels onto or down toward the floor. Straighten your knees but be sure not to lock them. Firm the outer thighs and roll the upper thighs inward slightly.

4. Firm the outer arms and from these two points, lift along your inner arms from the wrists to the tops of the shoulders. Firm your shoulder blades against your back, then widen them and draw them toward the tailbone. Keep the head between the upper arms while not letting it hang.

5. Hold the pose for five deep breaths as you inhale holding your breath for ten seconds, and then exhaling.

Homeostasis Yoga

Breath of fire with Seiken punches, five sets of ten, into hero pose for five deep breaths

1. Sitting in easy pose, engage in breath of fire.

2. At the same time, throw out karate punches straight as you punch alternating your left and right arms for five sets of ten.

3. After, transition into hero pose: get into a kneeling position. Your knees should be together, and your feet should be slightly wider than your hips. Keep the tops of your feet flat on the floor. (If this is uncomfortable, put a cushion or block under your buttocks, thighs, or calves.)

4. Place your hands on your thighs. Sit up straight to open your chest and lengthen your spine.

5. Do deep breathing for five breaths.

Breath of fire with tuck pose for 120 breaths, into upward facing dog and child pose for five deep breaths

1. Go into tuck pose while on your knees and your forehead near the floor as you cover your neck with your hands.

2. While in the tuck pose, do breath of fire for 120 consecutive breaths.

3. After, transition into upward facing dog.

4. Do deep breathing for one breath.

5. Go back into child pose for one deep breath.

6. Repeat the transition from upward facing dog to child pose four more times.

7. Child pose for five deep breaths

Mountain pose for five deep breaths

1. Stand with the big toes touching and a small amount of space between the heels.

2. Root down with the big toe mounds and pull up with the inner arches.

3. Press the thigh bones back while gently releasing the tailbone down.

4. Draw the shoulders back to align with the side body while softening the front ribs towards the frontal hipbones.

5. Stack the crown of the head above the pelvis with the chin level to the floor.

6. Press down through the four corners of each foot and lift up through the length of the body, ascending the crown of the head to the ceiling.

7. Hold this position for five deep breaths, holding your breath for ten seconds, and then releasing.

Breath of fire with muscle tension relaxation into corpse pose for two minutes

1. Lie on your back. In this exercise, you will tense each muscle group for ten seconds, and at the same time perform breathing exercises. After tensing the selected muscle group, do breath of fire, then when releasing the tension of the muscle, take one deep breath, hold your breath for ten seconds, and relax. The order is as follows.

2. Stretch your feet towards you tensing your feet, ankles, and calves, then release.

3. Tense your thighs and then release.

4. Squeeze your buttocks and hips and then release.

5. Suck in your stomach and then release.

6. Take a deep breath for your chest and hold. Do not do breath of fire here.

7. Push your shoulders up towards your ear and then release.

8. Stretch your neck by looking forward and hold the pose, then release.

9. Tighten your fists and curl them towards your elbow tightening your forearms as well and then release.

10. Tighten your triceps by turning your arms towards your body and then release.

11. Make a muscle pose, tightening your biceps and then release.

12. Make a sour face like you're sucking a lemon and release.

13. Make a look of surprise on your face and then release.

14. Return to normal breathing and relax into corpse pose: settle down on your back. Separate the feet as wide as your yoga mat, allowing the legs to fall open. Turn the palms to face the ceiling and rest the arms just far enough from the body so that they do not touch the torso.

15. Scan the body to notice if there are any asymmetries and adjust.

16. Let the eyes close and imagine them dropping back deeply into the sockets. Allow the muscles and bones to become heavy.

17. Notice if there are places that are still tense and use exhales to invite in a quality of release.

18. Gradually let the breath become softer and natural.

19. Continue to follow the breath so that the mind too becomes softer and quieter.

20. Rest deeply, without sleeping, for two minutes.

Two Ohm chants through deep breathing and closing meditation

1. While going back to easy pose, take a deep inhale, and then while exhaling, release the chant of "Ohm."

2. Take another deep inhale and do the chant one more time.

3. Go into prayer pose and give gratitude for another day.

....

After completing this sequence, begin your day. As you stimulate your nervous system daily, this opens you to be more available to the guided emotions of anger, fear, and indecision, and it also allows you to practice compassion, freedom, and empowered decision-making in your daily life. From a traditional top-down method, ratio-nalization and telling yourself something positive can help you to maintain and keep your feelings at bay while maintaining the status quo of your life. However, from this upside-down routine, you are giving yourself permission to let go and break out of your comfort zone, and through your emotions, evaluate the life that you are currently living.

In fact, after completing this routine for the first time, there will be a feeling of weirdness because there will be a separation from yourself and your own mind. In fact, you are practicing a more natural way of living, going from trying to conform to what you are supposed to be by constantly monitoring your thoughts, to a state of being free to discover who you really are and allowing yourself permission to feel emotions without any sense of guilt. This perspective places no restrictions on how you should feel and replaces preserving your self-esteem with finding meaning in your everyday experiences.

The upside-down method allows you to be as free as you want to be because you are sending the message to your nervous system that there is no danger in being naturally who you are in the first place. The only thing that you are doing now is undoing all of the restricted beliefs and acts of conformity that caused you so much pain in the first place. This is the preparation from going from consequence-based sympathetic thinking, to contemplative and parasympathetic processing.

The analogy of this approach is that you are a racehorse who has been locked in a barn for some time, which has forced you to suppress your strengths due to fear of consequences, and now you are finally set free to live the life that you want to live. With this freedom to run without restriction and roam new lands will also come a mixture of emotions that includes the empowered state you are now living in, as well as the pains that are still stored from the past. This will require you to navigate your course by prioritizing your new-found freedom of contemplative thinking through your parasympathetic structure over the past events and restrictions that were placed on you through consequence-based thinking through sympathetic reactions. This dual nature of expanding and growing, while at the same time mourning and healing are all within your grasp now, which represents the homeostasis of your whole nervous system structure.

Chapter 8

Using Guided Emotions

In this chapter, we will begin the process of using guided emotions in your everyday life. Guided emotions are triggered by the learned helplessness and feelings that are stored from the experiences of the past, which are then triggered by circumstances in your present-day situations, and which set the course for the direction you move in your life moving forward. The goal of a guided emotion is to take you out of the disappointed state of the sympathetic nervous system by leading you to identify the behaviors that are required of you to breakthrough and succeed.

Guided emotions can only go two ways: either you will use them externally which will lead to self-sabotaging behaviors as you continuously stay in the cycle of achieving an external answer, or you can be guided to internalize the situation and allow for the healing of a stored pain. When you experience a guided emotion, it is important to remember that the stronger the intensity of the emotion, the greater the opportunity there is to heal. More often than not, individuals will often mistake a guided emotion as being their own intuition, when actually it is nothing more than the pleasure sensors firing in the brain due to preparing for emotional pain. When I was working with a client who was struggling with depression due to doubt and anger about the core beliefs of her particular religion, she would often act in anger when discussing her depression and state that her intuition was telling her, "Satan is trying to take my mind right now!"

However, as we processed her guided emotions, the actual truth was that she wanted to explore a life outside of her particular faith and to feel okay about her desire to expand who she was. And through this process, she was able to get out of her negative filter and learned helpless beliefs to acknowledging her desire to be more independent and to expand the various areas of her life. As she shifted from a 10/90 of learned helplessness to a 90/10 space of empowerment, from that moment forward her guided emotion of pain allowed for her own intuition to be uncovered. In a metaphysical sense, intuition means following your gut, but if you are following your gut from a pained and helpless state, that is not your intuition at all. In fact, the greater the pain, the more chaotic it will feel emotionally because you are experiencing a nervous system triad of:

- the sympathetic nervous system seeking to react immediately

- the pleasure sensors firing in the brain to deal with emotional pain

- the racing thoughts of the mind to seek one perfect outcome.

So aside from the emotion that is being felt, when you bring in all of the components of the nervous system triad, the combination of it all can make it feel overwhelming. If you use a traditional top-down approach here, your focus will remain on the racing thoughts in your mind, and you would do your best to try to calm your mind down. The racing thoughts would come from consequence-based thinking as your sympathetic nervous system is trying to find out ways to avoid pain. In approaching it this way, it is the same as physiologically having a gun to your head as you are trying to rationalize at that moment, "Well, he hasn't shot me yet, so calm down." Trying to rationalize during a learned helpless response is very difficult because of the goal of containing the emotions due to the influence of the nervous system's involvement. And the more body-conscious one becomes, the more aware an individual will be regarding how much involvement the nervous system has when it comes to one's mental and emotional wellbeing. When you are able to do that, you are out of consequence-based thinking, and you have expanded to a state of contemplation where a bigger picture of your life can be seen. From the upside-down approach, it is recognizing the inner sensations in the nervous system triad and taking the danger out of the perceived situations. From that standpoint, you are dealing directly with the sympathetic nervous system and creating the awareness that:

- there is no external danger happening

- the consequence-based thinking through racing thoughts is not necessary

- you have the freedom of choice to break free now.

And as you go through your daily life, do your best to become more body-conscious and recognize those moments where the nervous system is involved. For example, if you feel like you need to complete a task immediately, but it is not required to do so, stop for a moment and recognize that this is just your sympathetic nervous system responding. Or if you are involved in a conversation with someone or watching a movie and you get that cringe sensation where you slightly feel embarrassed by the emotions emerging, recognize that this is simply the pleasure sensors in your brain firing. And finally, if your mind is racing at rapid speeds, be aware that there is no external solution required, no perfect solution needed, and no life-or-death scenario taking place that requires your mind to act this way.

This consequence-based thinking is all coming from the danger responses of the sympathetic nervous system. These moments of awareness will open the door for you to become more body-conscious and be more available to using an upside-down approach and mentally expanding out of fear of consequence-based thinking. In fact, the more aware you become of these sensations, the less association there will be with thoughts and circumstances causing your feelings. Those breaks in association will create more experiences of being present, feeling more centered, and seeing life in a more expanded and contemplative way.

Remember that each day that you live has so much importance because it holds the keys for you to go where you want to go. Every interaction, every circumstance, and every moment holds the opportunity to learn and grow, and ultimately to heal from the pains of your past. Throughout your day, situations in your life that are viewed as negative will try to reinforce why you chose to live in a state of disappointment, and it is important to avoid self-sabotaging behaviors. You will know when the temptation to go into self-sabotaging occurs because it will feel so right to do what is wrong. Once you act out you in learned helplessness, the increased sensations from the nervous system triad will only give you the boost and energy to continue in self-sabotage.

For example, if you use the guided emotion of anger outwardly and you start to yell and scream at everyone because it feels so right and justified, it is simply your pleasure sensors and nervous system on full display. And as the behaviors extend externally to blaming, criticizing, and telling long-winded stories about why your life is not working, the reinforcement of the learned helpless belief within takes place. Remember, you are better than that! On the flip side, as positive occurrences take place in your life that are leading you to your goals and dreams, remember a polarity will occur as your enthusiasm for life will emerge because you are going in that direction of success, and also at the same time, your nervous system reactions from learned helplessness will be coming out as well. This is the reflection of choosing success over not experiencing pain and the beginning of experiencing proprioception and contemplative thinking.

When using the guided emotions that are to be outlined, it is important to start your day from a 90/10 perspective. That means that you are living by:

- pursuing your dreams over seeking emotional safety

- choosing to expand out of consequence-based thinking into contemplation and expansive thinking

- remembering that all answers that you seek are all within you.

Also, it is important to remember that whenever you start to externalize by blaming or criticizing, that you go back to the finger-pointing analogy. The pointed finger represents the stimulus

(10%), while the three fingers pointing back at you represent the guided emotions (90%) of:

- Anger
- Fear
- Indecision.

In psychology, when working with clients, there are three basic states that are required to achieve success from a top-down point of view. The first stage is the contemplation stage, where clients explore the idea of changing their life. That extends to the second stage, which is preparation where the client starts planning the direction of their life. And lastly, the action stage is where direct action towards the goal is taken. This approach is based on changing your thinking first, which will then lead to a change of feelings and then finally, your actions. From an upside-down perspective, we use this change model in reverse.

We begin with the action stage, which will be triggered by your environment and will lead to one of your guided emotions emerging from your nervous system. From there, we go into the preparation stage as your pleasure sensors are turned on, which will enhance the guided emotion being felt, as we prepare to turn them off. Lastly, we go from thinking in consequences to contemplation as we are available to learn the lesson of empowerment that has emerged from this opportunity. Once you are in the contemplation stage, and you have internally addressed your guided emotion triggers, you are literally rewriting the story of your life, choice by choice. Each empowered and internal decision leads to letting go of the negative story that has been stored in your nervous system, and at the same time, a new narrative based on empowerment is being written every day. These three stages will be the upside-down plan that will be taken when the opportunity to heal emerges. Below are the three upside-down stages in-depth:

Level 1 – Sympathetic Reaction (Action)

Through the environmental trigger, the nervous system reaction of immediacy is activated along with one of the three guided emotions:

- Anger
- Fear
- Indecision.

Level 2 – Guided Emotion + Pleasure Sensors (Preparation)

The guided emotion, combined with the pleasure sensors in your brain, will create a more intense feeling due to preparing to deal with pain from the external environment.

- Example: Anger + Pleasure Sensors = Resentment

- Example: Fear + Pleasure sensors = Anxiety

- Example: Indecision + Pleasure sensors = Freaking out.

Level 3 – Racing Thoughts (Contemplation)

The racing thoughts that are occurring, as one perfect outcome is sought due to the danger response being on and being in consequence-based thinking. It is here that the reframing from a 10/90 to a 90/10 approach can take place through the appropriate action.

....

As we go through each guided emotion more in-depth, the three levels of action or stages will be identified to help you break out of the disappointed state of the sympathetic nervous system. It is also important to remember that the closer you are to your goals and dreams, the greater the danger response that will occur due to the learned helpless pain that wants to come out. This polarity is inevitable and cannot be avoided. It is remembering in these moments that you are strong enough to handle the polarity of embracing your success while mourning and releasing the stored pains of the past.

Guided Emotion 1: Anger

Anger comes from being upset due to perceived external circumstances because you are not internally acknowledging that the negative characteristics you see in others are actually within you, and you are defending and protecting old belief systems about yourself that no longer serve you. Anger is a guided emotion because it is triggered by your fight response, and the goal is to protect and preserve what you have. It is a survival state reaction where you are outwardly assertive in your actions of criticizing, judging, and blaming others, while inwardly you are completely passive in your own pursuit of success because of the belief that you cannot have it.

From an emotional standpoint, this form of protection when used outwardly creates only greater pain and suffering to yourself and to those around you. When you externalize anger, you are in consequence-based thinking, as you are protecting and defending the pain that you feel inside as well as your limited belief about yourself. Every justification you externalize to others then internalizes the belief that you need to emotionally survive and that you have not found your external answer yet. In this perceived need to fight, you will argue with others about right and wrong, you will try to convince and force others to your point of view, and ultimately be in a judgmental space where everything has to be proven to you.

If you are deeply in the throes of anger because of learned helplessness, you will argue about being right even though deep down, you know you are wrong. When used internally, however, the emotion will first lead you to identify and stop the behaviors that are keeping you in a negative filter of depression, and secondly show you, through others, the characteristics and limited belief systems that you need to stop defending.

Once the guided emotion of anger is triggered through your circumstances, it is important to do the following:

Level 1 – Sympathetic Reaction (Action):

Shift from anger to compassion to stop the sympathetic reaction of immediacy.

Level 2 – Anger + Pleasure Sensors (Preparation):

Shut off the pleasure sensors in your brain by going 90/10 and by acknowledging that there is nothing to fight for or protect. Emotions will enhance to:

- resentment
- rage
- jealousy.

Level 3 – Racing Thoughts (Contemplation):

Stop the racing thoughts by acknowledging the learned helpless behavior. Statements include:

- "I will stop being negative and critical because I now see it in myself."

- "My jealousy towards that person is because I seek that level of success for myself."

....

Working with guided emotions in this way takes practice, but after a while, it becomes easier and easier to do. Also, as you go through this process every day and you start to write down the occurrences, you will see the patterns of the past, the current lessons to be learned, as well as the future decisions that are required to set you free.

When working with clients, I had each client write down the daily guided emotions that they were experiencing and to bring it back to sessions. Below is Amy's daily log when it came to anger, and just from the three examples provided, it was clear the learned helpless emotions that needed to be healed, as well as the choices she needed to make to get out of the negative filter of depression. Below is a sample of working with anger:

Event 1: Talking to Darrell at work annoys the shit out of me because all he does is complain and bring everyone down.

Level 1 – Sympathetic Reaction (Action):
I show compassion to Darrell and myself because we are both doing the best that we can.

Level 2 – Anger + Pleasure Sensors
(Preparation):
I go 90/10 by acknowledging that I feel rage at myself because I complain and can bring people down.

Level 3 – Racing Thoughts (Contemplation):
I choose to stop complaining about my life and bringing others down. I empower myself to do so.

> **Event 2:** My friend Mike always calls me when he has problems, and he is so dependent upon me.

Level 1 – Sympathetic Reaction (Action):
I show compassion to Mike and myself because we are both doing the best that we can.

Level 2 – Anger + Pleasure Sensors
(Preparation):
I go 90/10 by acknowledging that I am resentful at myself because I can be emotionally dependent upon other people by using their problems to not deal with mine.

Level 3 – Racing Thoughts (Contemplation):
I choose to stop being dependent on others by controlling them and focus my attention on improving myself by being more independent.

> **Event 3:** My supervisor, when she presents at meetings, thinks she is all that just because she went to school. I have more experience than she, and I should be in that position.

Level 1 – Sympathetic Reaction (Action):
I show compassion to my supervisor and myself because we are both doing the best that we can.

Level 2 – Anger + Pleasure Sensors (Preparation):
I go 90/10 by acknowledging that I am jealous of my supervisor because I desire to get my degree and have a position like her.

Level 3 – Racing Thoughts (Contemplation):

I choose to stop being jealous of her and celebrate her success. I will ask her about where she went to school.

....

Amy, through this process, was able to break free from the negative cycles of complaining, using her friends as an excuse, and being jealous of her supervisor. Once she internalized those moments, she was able to break the learned helpless emotions within her and empower herself to go back to school and get her degree. She broke away from the negative filters associated with survival and protection, and she began to explore what was possible in her life through her environment teaching her.

Amy, after this process, shared how she would be the first person in her family to go to college and get a graduate degree, and that she has been living in that level of restriction her whole life. Stored in her sympathetic nervous system was the protective belief that "It is impossible for me to go to school, and I will need to make do with what I have." However, through her guided emotions of anger and use of contemplation and expanded thinking, Amy was led to the empowered path of getting her degree and obtaining a higher-paid position.

Guided Emotion 2: Fear

Fear is the perceived helpless feeling associated with not being able to handle an external event and the belief that you need to escape that situation. More specifically, you are in consequence-based thinking as you are externally running from triggers that you believe that are emotionally dangerous for you, but in truth, you need to internally run to the magnificent traits and qualities that are already within you, which is where your safety is.

Fear is a guided emotion because it is triggered by your flee response, and the goal is to run away from a dangerous circumstance due to the belief that it cannot be handled. It is a survival reaction because of the fear of being dominated by a circumstance, and when expressed outwardly from an emotional standpoint, the actions become trying to mind-read what other people are thinking, trying to predict outcomes before they occur, and going through racing thoughts of "What if" in the attempt to establish some sense of control.

In this flee response through fear, individuals will often avoid situations, make a lot of excuses for not doing something, and stay in the negative filter of helplessness because emotional safety needs to be guaranteed for that person before trying anything. However, when you go within and use the guided emotion of fear, you will actually realize that, internally, you are actually running from your own suppressed strengths and talents that are within you. That is why when fear is internalized, you break out of the external thought processes of consequence-based thinking, and transition to an expansive, contemplative state, where you can truly cultivate your gifts and skills that have not been allowed to flourish.

From an external consequence point of view, it can be viewed as the event that is being avoided, but in truth through contemplation, it is the internal need to run to your own unique and independent abilities. When the environment triggers the guided emotion of fear, it is important to:

Level 1 – Sympathetic Reaction (Action):

Shift from Fear to Freedom to stop the sympathetic reaction of immediacy.

Level 2 – Fear + Pleasure Sensors (Preparation):

Shut off the pleasure sensors in your brain by going 90/10 and by acknowledging that there is no danger to run from. Emotions will enhance to:

- anxiety
- dread
- suspense.

Level 3 – Racing Thoughts (Contemplation):

Stop the racing thoughts by acknowledging the learned helpless behavior:

- "There is no emotional danger to run from in this event that is triggering me."

- "I exercise my freedom of choice and run to all of my assertive qualities and talents right now!"

....

When working with the client who suffered from social anxiety in the previous chapter, he was consistently fixated on the fact that he had difficulty in social situations due to a lack of confidence and because he was socially inept. However, as he worked through his guided emotions of fear, he was actually able to discover the opposite was true. I had him write down daily the circumstances that triggered his fears and bring them back to sessions. Here is what he had come up with:

Event 1: Going on a set-up date tomorrow with my friend, and I am so worried about looking like a fool.

Level 1 – Sympathetic Reaction (Action):
I exercise my freedom to enjoy myself and be who I am and allow my date to have the same freedom to enjoy herself as well.

Level 2 – Fear + Pleasure Sensors (Preparation):
I go 90/10 by acknowledging the anxiety triggered by this date represents me no longer suppressing my desire to connect with another person and to be involved in a relationship.

Level 3 – Racing Thoughts (Contemplation):
I choose to run to the great qualities within me that I have as a potential partner and loving person that I am.

Event 2: Class presentation, as I am afraid of coming across as weak and looking stupid. I fear being judged and told that I am no good.

Level 1 – Sympathetic Reaction (Action):
I exercise my freedom to present information in a kind, gentle and assertive way and allow the class the freedom to receive the information.

Level 2 – Fear + Pleasure Sensors (Preparation):
I go 90/10 by acknowledging the feeling of dread triggered by this presentation. This dread represents me no longer suppressing my strengths in presenting information in my own unique and individual way.

Level 3 – Racing Thoughts (Contemplation):
I exercise my freedom of choice and allow my natural skill set of presenting information to emerge freely and openly.

> **Event 3:** Going back home to see my mom on the weekend. She constantly criticizes me and tells me what I am doing wrong all of the time. Whenever I confront her about her actions, she then acts out and tells me how ungrateful I am. I hate the feeling of suspense around her.

Level 1 – Sympathetic Reaction (Action):
I exercise my freedom to be my own person and allow my mother to be the same.

Level 2 – Fear + Pleasure Sensors (Preparation):
I go 90/10 by acknowledging the suspense of criticism triggered by being with my mom represents me allowing my independence to be who I desire to be to come out all of the time now. I no longer have to try and be what she wants me to be.

Level 3 – Racing Thoughts (Contemplation):
I exercise my freedom of choice and run to all my strengths which are: kindness, gentleness, confidence, desire to connect and to be accepted for who I am, my assertive side, my human side because I make mistakes, and to give permission to be me and grow every single day!

This client, through internalizing his guided emotions of fear, was able to break through by allowing his strengths and talents to emerge which he had been holding back for most of his life. The reason that he was suppressing all of his great independent qualities was because that was the requirement of him to continue to have a relationship with his mother, as well as emotionally survive and make it livable in that household before he left for college.

The client before college had to focus on his mother's feelings at all times, and he fixated on not making mistakes and not asserting himself too much because if he did, she would act out at him and blame him for her unhappiness. His actual fear of mistakes was nothing more than the fear of allowing his independence to emerge around his mom instead of remaining docile. That is why when he was met with social triggers away from his mother, like presenting in class and going out on dates, it was those internal pains of trying to please others and trying to be perfect that were emerging from him because he was struggling to freely express his independent nature. And once he expanded into contemplative thinking, all of those racing thoughts about looking dumb, stupid, and embarrassing himself stopped.

As the client continuously worked through his guided emotions of fear daily and stabilized his nervous system, he contemplated how far he came and brought a list to session one week. The list was broken down into two categories that included how he was supposed to be versus who he really was. The list is below:

Old Self

- Submissive
- Perfectionistic
- Pleasing
- No mistakes
- Live for others
- Non-emotional
- Manly

Real Self

- Independent
- Kind
- Sensitive
- Positive
- Enthusiastic
- Desire to belong and be a part of
- Confident

- Reflective
- Silly
- Hopeful
- Loving
- Complex
- Understanding
- Open
- Loving

His old self represented how he saw life through his sympathetic consequence-based thinking, while his real self displayed his parasympathetic and contemplative nature that lived in his true independent state. He was able to break the learned helpless feelings that came from his anxiety due to his upbringing and establish a new foundation for himself that was completely free from his past and based upon his present through his choice of freedom. And as he continued on, I am sure that his list of who he is now is getting even longer, as he continues to live in an expanded mental and emotional state.

Guided Emotion 3: Indecision

Indecision reflects the mixed emotions that one feels because it involves the need to let go of the negative aspects of their life in order to make more empowered choices. That is why emotions are jumbled because a sorting-through of the helpless beliefs and feelings need to be let go so that the more empowered decisions can be made. This starts with letting go of:

- the negative filter associated with depression

- the negative filter associated with anxiety

- circumstances and people who are negatively influencing you.

Indecision from a nervous system standpoint comes from your freeze response, and it is associated with the last resort. When, from a physical danger standpoint, you are unable to fight and protect yourself, nor are you able to run from the situation, the body completely freezes and plays dead in hopes that you will be ignored and left alone.

From a reptilian point of view, this response is seen as the weakest and most helpless out of all three nervous system responses, but in the context of the nervous system as a whole, it is actually the most evolved.

This response comes from the desire to not dominate or be dominated, but rather to seek a more long-term outcome that is more peaceful. From an emotional context, indecision represents the dual nature that comes from surviving through your sympathetic nervous system to the purpose of life reflections from your parasympathetic structure and the expanded mental and emotional state that encompasses it all.

From an evolutionary point of view, indecision through mixed emotions comes from your altruistic and conscientiousness side that desires a good life for everyone, including yourself. This more evolved state sees survival from the viewpoint of a higher state of consciousness that goes beyond just survival. For example, when it comes to promoting world peace, would you want your leader to have a reptilian "lead, follow, or get out of the way" mentality, or would you want someone who was more in a reflective state and took more time processing before making decisions?

That is what indecision represents from a quality-of-life standpoint, which is the expanded and emotional range to let go of old survival beliefs, in exchange for more evolved and empowered decisions.

When the guided emotion of indecision is triggered by your environment, the upside-down approach is below:

Level 1 – Sympathetic Reaction (Action):

Shift from Indecision to Letting Go of all that does not serve you to stop the sympathetic reaction of immediacy.

Level 2 – Indecision + Pleasure Sensors (Preparation):

Shut off the pleasure sensors in your brain by going 90/10 and by acknowledging that indecision is nothing more than me being open and receptive at that moment:

- uncertainty
- doubt
- vacillation.

Level 3- Racing Thoughts (Contemplation):

Stop the racing thoughts by acknowledging the empowered choice:

- "I choose to treat myself with self-respect."

- "I choose to set boundaries with my family."

....

The environmental trigger of indecision will come when the empowered choice is clouded with the mixture of emotions that are involved in one's past. It is important here to work through the mixture of emotions by letting go of the negative filter beliefs first. When working with Jim, the client who was discussed in the first chapter, he was guided by indecision and led to the empowered decisions that needed to be made. Below are Jim's triggers for indecision.

Event 1: Deciding whether or not I should quit my job because of its stability even though I am not happy here. I am not sure how my wife will take it either.

Level 1 – Sympathetic Reaction (Action):
I acknowledge the mixed emotions within me and choose to let go of all limiting beliefs regarding my job.

Level 2 – Indecision + Pleasure Sensors (Preparation):
I go 90/10 by acknowledging the uncertainty I feel and let go of:

- *The belief that I cannot find another job*

- *The belief that my wife won't understand and will hate me.*

Level 3 – Racing Thoughts (Contemplation):
I choose to stop the uncertainty by redoing my CV and looking for a new job, as well as discussing my plans with my wife. I empower myself to make choices that are good for me.

Event 2: Deciding whether to bring up the topic of wanting to see a couple's therapist with my wife. My wife might get upset, and I do not want to look like I am blaming her for my unhappiness.

Level 1 – Sympathetic Reaction (Action):
I acknowledge the mixed emotions within me and choose to let go of all limiting beliefs regarding my wife.

Level 2 – Indecision + Pleasure Sensors (Preparation):

I go 90/10 by acknowledging the doubt I feel and let go of:

- the belief that I am hurting my wife by wanting to go to couple's therapy

- the belief that my opinion does not matter and that I have no say.

Level 3 – Racing Thoughts (Contemplation):

I choose to stop the doubt by making the decision to talk to my wife about couples' therapy and to work with my therapist in having the discussion with her. I might even bring her into my individual session so that she can get a feel for what therapy is like.

Event 3: Going to the gym and beginning the process of losing twenty pounds instead of going to happy hour with my friends. My doctor told me that I might have to take blood pressure medication if I do not get my weight down.

Level 1 – Sympathetic Reaction (Action):
I acknowledge the mixed emotions within me and choose to let go of all limiting beliefs and excuses associated with exercise.

Level 2 – Indecision + Pleasure Sensors (Preparation):
I go 90/10 by acknowledging the vacillation I feel and let go of:

- *the belief that I do not have time to work out*

- *the belief that it is too late for me to start now*

- *the belief that I will lose my friends if I do not go to happy hour with them.*

Level 3 – Racing Thoughts (Contemplation):
I choose to stop the vacillation by doing the one-week free trial membership at my local gym, and I will start tomorrow. I empower myself by taking care of my body as well as offering the opportunity to my friends.

....

Jim, when he learned to let go of his limiting beliefs and actions that did not serve him, opened the door for the empowered decisions that were always available to him. Once he let go of the excuses, the narrow beliefs about his job prospects, his wife, and the letting go of happy hour and alcohol, Jim mentally, emotionally, and physically improved his overall quality of life.

Through the guided emotion of indecision, Jim made the empowered decisions to find a better job that he was happier at, to go to couples' therapy with his wife which immensely improved the quality of their relationship, and to go to the gym where he lost weight and was overall in better health. Jim's empowered decisions lead to his greater success.

In closing, all three guided emotions of anger, fear, and indecision will lead you to get out of learned helplessness and to go towards an empowered path to healing and achieving success. At each triggered and guided moment, through anger you are able to break from the negative cycles and behaviors associated with any depressive symptoms you may have. Similarly, through fear you have the opportunity to break free from the helpless cycle of anxiety by allowing all of the great qualities that you have been holding back to emerge in your life. And finally, when it comes to moments of indecision, the empowered choice is available through filtering through the mixed emotions by letting go of that which does not serve you and evolving towards a quality of life that is reflective of your dreams.

Chapter 9

Contemplative Meditation

Meditation has long been a tool used to facilitate deep thinking and self-reflection, and it can be done in various forms. For many years, meditation and contemplation were used synonymously, and up until the last few decades, the term *contemplative meditation* would have been perceived as one and the same. Today, however, the definition of contemplative meditation does serve a practical purpose. To understand what contemplative meditation is, it is important to understand the purpose of it. The goal is to promote deep thought and inspire insight, which is contrary to the concept of having no thoughts at all.

The Latin origins of contemplation and meditation both have similarities but also visible differences which highlight how different this form of meditation can be. To understand the distinction and to eliminate confusion between contemplation and meditation, it is important to understand their original meanings. The word contemplation is the combination of the Latin prefix con and root templum, which means "being with the shrine or sacred place." Temples were often at higher viewpoints in the landscape, allowing one to observe from higher ground. Therefore, combining the various root definitions, the word contemplation can be defined as the act of seeing or observing with the help of the divine in an expanded and elevated space.

The word meditate is derived from the Latin verb meditor which means "pondering, considering and studying," which in and of itself has no real spiritual component to it. Contemplation is actually the more spiritually derived action, where meditation represents the more systematic and rational exploration of the questions about life.

Often times, this leads to confusion regarding contemplative meditation and mindfulness meditation. Mindfulness meditation revolves around the idea of non-attachment to one's thoughts, feelings, circumstances, and things. The goal is to have thoughtless awareness where the mind is completely clear and available to each and every present moment. The widespread popularization of mindfulness can get confused with thinking that meditation is the practice of clearing the mind of all thoughts, when in fact, the true meaning of meditation is to purposefully engage in deep thought. So, in terms of its original use in describing a state of divine observation or inner listening, contemplation is a spiritual process of focused deliberation. In order to understand how to practice contemplative meditation, it is important to understand how to define it.

Contemplative meditation can be defined as a spiritually focused observation or consideration of a specific idea, question, or situation, with the goal of receiving insight from the inner wisdom or the divine within. Therefore, the purpose of contemplative meditation is to seek answers to specific questions from whatever your concept of a higher power is. The practice of contemplative meditation can be used to assist in making big life decisions, and as you go through your day, your guided emotions can help lead you to contemplate the higher purpose for your life.

As you get to the night, you can use contemplative meditation by asking yourself and reflecting upon the questions that are below. Each question comes from the three guided emotions that you experienced throughout your day, as well as expanding your parasympathetic desires and views of your life.

What limiting beliefs were brought to my attention today that I no longer need to protect or defend? (Anger to Compassion)

The question comes from your experiences with the guided emotion of anger and utilizing a 90/10 approach by using compassion. Through the external triggers that took place during the day, you can identify the limiting beliefs and behaviors that you are engaging in and compassionately choose to stop the behaviors. This form of reflection and contemplation allows for the getting out of the state of disappointment by opening your parasympathetic nervous system as you release the stored emotions that come from your own limiting beliefs about your life. Oftentimes, if you can get out of the sympathetic state of right or wrong and "should have" and "could have," anger is usually a sign that your current life situation is no longer serving you and that there is something greater out there for you.

To expand into this parasympathetic space, you need to internally open yourself up and become available to what is possible for your life outside of your current circumstance. Most people will use that emotion to defend and stay in the same circumstance based on consequence-based thinking, but it takes contemplation to understand that your life is seeking to progress beyond the current circumstances that you are living in.

Self-sabotaging behaviors with anger involve fighting for your right to stay in a dysfunctional environment and tirelessly trying to make it work, versus opening yourself up to moving on because you are evolving as a human being. This phase of expansion requires you to let go of all limiting beliefs which are reinforced by the anger you feel towards those that trigger you. The guided emotion of anger leads you to compassion, which then opens the door for your what your life possibilities are to be next, to then expanding out of your current circumstances.

What gifts and talents do I need to cultivate more based on the freedom I exercised today? (Fear to Freedom)

This question comes from the guided emotion of fear, and when you utilize the 90/10 approach of freedom, you become more open to see the gifts, talents, and abilities that are seeking to emerge from you. This is where you get to release the person that was being pigeonholed into living up to a standard that others wanted you to be, by allowing yourself to live in true freedom to be who you really are, whether you are accepted or not. This provides you permission to get in touch with your independence and your uniqueness as an individual. When you contemplate the lessons of fear here, it is important to invert how you see fear. The external circumstance is nothing but the trigger that shows you internally what talents you need run to and cultivate more.

Being an individual is experiencing all parts of who you are, and where there is great fear, beneath lies great talent and abilities waiting to be honed and sharpened. For example, when people say I am introverted or extroverted, that is just a sympathetic way of pigeonholing yourself from an all-or-nothing perspective. The truth is all people are both introverted and extroverted, and depending upon situations and the people they are around, the various spectrum of introvert and extrovert can be seen. The guided emotion of fear leads to freedom, which then opens the door for you to be all aspects of who you are.

What are the aspects of my life that I need to let go of based upon choosing empowerment? (Indecision to Empowerment)

This question addresses the guided emotion of indecision due to the mixture of emotions that are taking place within, and through a 90/10 approach of choosing empowerment, allows for you to let go of the areas of your life that no longer serve you. This can include limiting beliefs and behaviors, as well as circumstances and individuals in your life. By letting go of that which no longer serves you, it opens the door to being available for living the life that you always wanted to live.

Out of the three guided emotions, this is the most evolved because it requires you to see from a complete expanded mental and emotional space, and it is the transition point of having your parasympathetic nervous system take over your emotional world. Through contemplation of your mixed emotions of indecision, you are slowly releasing the sympathetic structure from your emotional world, and you are increasing the influence and activity of your parasympathetic system.

Empowerment starts with letting go of the areas of your life that are holding you back, which then opens the door to empowered decision-making based upon wholeness and prosperity. Empowerment is the constant state of being in a mentally and emotionally expanded state, and through contemplation, choosing a life of quality over a life of survival. At this point, you have found the meaning required to come to terms with the painful areas of your life, as well as opening up yourself to the possibilities of what your life can be.

What did I learn about my life today that can be used towards pursuing my dreams?

- **(Compassion)** What expanded belief(s) about my life am I willing to accept now?

- **(Freedom)** What trait(s) did I display today that shows how independent I am?

- **(Empowerment)** What are the empowered belief(s) about my life that I need to start embracing now?

This is where you can use contemplation and meditation to reflect upon seeing the potential of your life. Throughout this whole upside-down day, you have reworked your whole psychological structure and have opened up and increased your parasympathetic nervous system. At this point, your sympathetic structure is continuously being removed from your emotional world, and it can be seen as the perceived emotional dangers that are no longer threatening. Also, as you continue on, the state of living in disappointment diminishes, and the heavy feelings around the head and chest begin to dissipate. Also, any heavy sensations in the head, similar to the bee buzzing feeling, reduce as buoyancy and mental clarity slowly become the norm. These questions, through your contemplative state, open the door for you to be available to your own intuition, and allow for you to go in the direction of your dreams.

Through the use of contemplative meditation, you are allowed to put together your whole day from an upside-down perspective and utilize your mind to focus upon what really matters in your life. You are no longer living in the limited paradigm of consequence-based thinking stemming from your sympathetic nervous system and now have expanded to seeing your life in a bigger context, as your parasympathetic structure is allowing contemplative thought to dominate your emotional life.

Once you get to the nighttime, you have created the condition for your mind to be used as a tool that benefits you in the pursuit of your dreams, versus living in a state of getting by and living in disappointment. From the morning where you begin the practice of regulating your nervous system, to the day where you use your guided emotions to teach and lead you, to the nighttime where your parasympathetic nervous system is fully active as well as your pineal gland, your mind is properly prepared to contemplate the direction and meaning of your life. And every day as you go through this upside-down cycle, you are opening yourself up to living the life that you have always deserved to live.

Chapter 10

Putting It All Together

When it comes to using this upside-down approach, it is the inverse of everything that you have been told throughout your life. In fact, it is the opposite of how I treated clients using traditional methods as well as how I used to deal with myself. Just like everyone else, I would go top-down, doing my best to hold myself together every day and to not let my emotions get out of hand. I would use rationalizations as my primary tool when dealing with myself, and for extended periods of time, it would work until it wouldn't. When anger came, I would defend my choice to live exactly the way I had been living, even though it was not making me happy, because I had to be right, no matter what.

Even when well-intentioned individuals who would see greater potential in me than I saw in myself tried to help me, I would push them aside, as I would gravitate to the other haters of life because I thought I was keeping it real. And when the feelings of fear came, I would constantly have racing thoughts, seeking to avoid situations to try and not experience those feelings again, even though it never worked. And finally, as all of my mixed emotions from indecision would all be inside of me because of my internal desire to expand my capacities, I would use my sympathetic thinking and shrink myself by pushing down my dreams and desires to seek emotional comfort and safety due to fear of consequences.

My emotional life mimicked living in physical danger every day as I was in survival mode, viewing life in a negative filter and living cautiously. I held the personal pains of my past close to me, and that stored pain and the work of the sympathetic nervous system kept me in a survival state. And in those moments where my emotions would take over my ability to rationalize, I would see it as having a breakdown, and my thoughts would race with "What is wrong with you?" to "What if you fail?" and "You are going to disappoint everyone around you!" My pleasure sensors would validate my lifestyle choices by enhancing my boldness to live in emotional safety or disappointment, and my disappointing choices in life would reflect my loyalty to safety.

This was my feeble attempt to maintain mental control of my life and be what I was supposed to be. It was a mask of perceived mental control that saw emotions as the enemy, and internally I was living in my own emotional jungle. In a real jungle, your sympathetic structure has to compare yourself to other animals around you for survival purposes to see how you can survive. However, in my emotional world, I was doing the same, but instead of comparing the speed and physical strength of myself and a tiger, I would compare myself to others in regard to income, how I was perceived, and the status of my occupation.

This style of living was the emotional jungle I lived in because my sympathetic world completely took over. This takeover led to greater depression and anxiety, which let me know that emotional safety for me was accomplished. It wasn't until I stopped the top-down method of seeking self-worth and started the upside-down approach of honoring my emotions that my life changed. I was seeing the nervous system's association with my feelings as well as my mind, and that paradoxical approach expanded my ability to see my life and world in a completely different way.

When I was working with clients using this method at the infancy stage of this project, it would be hit-or-miss, where some individuals would hate the whole experience, saying, "What the fuck is this?" while others would have tremendous breakthroughs, saying, "This has totally changed my life." It took years of research, practice, and implementation before a consistent outcome occurred, and life-changing moments became the norm. And the reason it became the norm was that every strong emotion, every chaotic impulse, and every danger response from each client was honored for what it was: a signpost for a breakthrough. And so, with that, I want to leave you with three things to remember about the upside-down approach:

#1 Take the sympathetic structure out of your emotional world.

In doing this, you are seeing anxiety and depression for what it is, being and living in complete and total emotional safety. From an upside-down lens, self-esteem is nothing more than self-preservation, and it is understanding that there is nothing to preserve in your emotional world. Using the sympathetic triad yoga along with embracing all of the emotional aspects of your life that you view as dangerous will eventually help you to remove that structure from this part of your world. Also, as you engage in parasympathetic and homeostasis yoga, your whole nervous system will stabilize as you will increase your parasympathetic activity in your daily living, increase the GABA receptors that go to your brain, and you will open up your pineal gland. All of this will get you out of the life-or-death, black-or-white, and all-or-nothing thinking associated with consequence-based thinking. At that point, you will not need to discipline your mind into forced positivity, but rather through your upside-down work, it will naturally take place because your parasympathetic structure has taken over your quality of life.

#2 Let your emotional world guide you instead of viewing it as the enemy.

All three guided emotions that come from your nervous system structure are here to serve you, and if you internalize the process and see its association with your nervous system, you can not only heal the pains of your past, but you can also transcend beyond it for a better future. Anger comes from the natural survival instinct to protect what you have, and its focus is not on anything else. From an upside-down context, if you can use that anger to identify the behaviors and the stored pain that is keeping you from moving forward, then you can set yourself free to start focusing on what your life could be. Anger, if internalized, can guide you to see the quality of life that you want to live, and it can help you to break the internal blockages in your life that are stopping you from getting it. The second guided emotion, fear, comes from the survival instinct of running away when it is believed that a situation cannot be handled through fighting, and this instinct is seeking another peripheral skillset from you to enhance survival. When it comes to your quality world, the premise is the same, as it is seeking your inner gifts and talents within you that have not been fully developed.

For example, if you are fearful of taking responsibility for your life, then fear is guiding you to that dormant responsible person within you to emerge. If you fear social situations, then the fear is guiding you to develop that part of yourself that truly desires to connect with others. And overall, if you are fearful of life, then the fear is internally guiding you to be that truly courageous person that you are. When it comes to indecision or mixed emotions, this evolved approach is seeking for you to think just beyond survival and to see more long-term solutions.

From a nervous system standpoint, this is the introduction of your parasympathetic structure as your job here is to let go of the lesser for the greater. More specifically, you are breaking away from consequence-based thinking into contemplative and expansive thinking. In a survival state, you would need to let go of all actions and surroundings that would limit your ability to survive and exchange them for the behaviors and circumstances that would enhance your ability to live.

Similarly, in your quality world, you would need to let go of all limiting behaviors, individuals and circumstances in your life that are holding you back, and exchange them for positive actions, supportive people and healthy surroundings that will enhance your quality of life.

#3 Use contemplation over rationalization.

The basic premise here is to get out of your head. Rationalizations are great when it comes to dealing with facts, and it is a completely an intellectual process. However, when it comes to your emotional world, at its best it is something that can help you to emotionally settle down, and at its worst, it is a dismissive and condescending approach to your own feelings. Statements when it comes to feelings like, "It is not happening now," and "Hold yourself together" can from a rational context be seen as helpful statements, or they can be seen as basically being told to stop acting crazy. When looking at depression and anxiety from a top-down perspective, it is using your mind as your guide, and the ultimate tool is to rationalize your way out of the symptoms of negative thinking. From an upside-down approach, negative thinking is viewed as the product of your sympathetic structure using the negative filter and helpless viewpoint for safety reasons, and so it is a matter of not rationalizing, but rather contemplating why your body has gone into this state.

Feelings from a top-down external context can be viewed as irrational, but from an internal and upside-down view, it is a necessary component to life. Rationalizations often require you to separate yourself from your feelings, and it can solely become a mind-centric activity. However, contemplation is different, because it does not view the mind as the be-all and end-all, but rather a collaborative partner that uses emotions and the nervous system structure as valuable information to use. Your nighttime use of contemplation will open the door and help you to uncover the more meaningful aspects of your life, and it will overall replace the incessant racing thoughts that come from your sympathetic world. And as your parasympathetic structure becomes more active in your quality world, the more expanded your level of contemplation becomes.

Benefits

When it comes to using this method, I have been so blessed to have been able to share this approach and to be a part of this process of helping others live a better life. It is a structured approach in the sense that every day is set up for you to find meaning and purpose, and it leads you to do the inner work to find the answers you seek. Once you implement this approach, no day is wasted because your nervous system responses, your emotional processes, and your use of contemplation are all about supporting you and leading you out of where you do not want to be. You become your own life coach as you use the information that you receive daily and let it guide you towards a better future. Consistently, I have heard about these four benefits from clients who have used this system:

"I'm finally living naturally as me."

This has been stated over and over by my clients as they share how they can just be themselves. The epiphany for many was how they were living their lives trying to be what they thought they should be, versus just living as they are. There is no second-guessing everything when it comes to their feelings, and a high level of emotional and mental freedom has emerged. Overall, there has been genuine and sincere gratitude in being able to live naturally as their unique, individual selves.

"My stress levels have reduced significantly."

Clients have shared continuously how much their level of stress has gone down. It has been stated repeatedly that what used to cause them great distress in their lives is not seen as a big deal anymore. Whether it is a supposed big meeting, or a work deadline, or a conflict with a partner or friend, it is all seen as not that big of a deal. It does not mean that they are neglecting their responsibilities or that they do not care, but it means they are being responsible without being neurotic, and their overall ability to multi-task and deal with life has become a greater skill. Through the direct action of stimulating the nervous system, as well as internalizing guided emotions, the clients have much higher levels of coping, and they often end up being the source of comfort to their friends and family members because of their more relaxed nature.

"I value myself and my beliefs more than what others think of me."

Clients have shared this consistently because this upside-down approach places a great deal of responsibility on yourself to live your best life. Your emotions are valued, and every peripheral contribution from your body is honored and explored. A common theme here is that those who used to believe that they needed validation for their past pains from their family members or friends have now transitioned to not really needing a lot of validation at all.

The reason for this is that through this method, you are validating all of your feelings every day, as well as healing the pains of your past. One client shared how they used to obsess about their reputation, whereas now, it really does not matter how she is perceived. She shared, "I am so busy focusing on my emotions and where they are trying to lead me, that the time-consuming activity of worrying about others has gone away." Choosing an upside-down life is truly the embodiment of holistic living.

"My quality of life has improved."

This has been said over and over again, and it has been shared that "My brand-new inner world is now reflected in my outer world." All of the inner work the clients did on themselves, the accountability and dedication to honor their emotions every day and to have the conviction to see it all the way through, changed their inner quality world, and that directly correlated to a new outer quality world. I have heard many times over how they have a new life that includes new friends, a new job, a new partner, and overall, a better outlook on life. It touches my heart when I hear statements like, "I cannot believe the life I am living now," "This is truly the life of my dreams," and "I laugh at who I used to be before."

I take so much pride in seeing the end results of hard work and ultimately seeing them honor the existence of their own lives. There is the saying, "When you look within, you no longer look without," and that is what the upside-down approach is. I thank you so much for taking the time to read this book, and I am so excited and thrilled for what lies ahead for you, as you transition to upside-down living.

Acknowledgements

First of all, I am so thankful for how this book came to be because it just felt like everything in the Universe was aligning accordingly. When this book project started, I had so many detailed notes about what this book was going to look like and how it was going to go. However, through this process, what this actually turned out to be was a truly spiritual endeavor that took every aspect and every detail of my life, tying in all of the work, knowledge and practice that I have done in my career, and then became represented in this work. When I signed with That Guy's House, I was not sure what to expect, but when I met CEO Sean Patrick for the first time, it was the perfect partnership. One aspect that bonded us instantly was our desire and passion for the self-help industry and how well-read we both were when it came to that field. Sean became my mentor on this book project, and through this collaboration, it weaved academic work, spiritual work, psychology, the art of storytelling, as well as discussions on life issues and what real healing meant to both of us. I am so thankful to Sean for not only being a mentor on this project, but a great friend, and I look forward to the future collaborations that are in store!

Thank you to everyone who has been a part of this book process, from Jesse who edited the book, to Sarah and Emma who helped with the press, to Leah who has created the most amazing design, and to Qi who took the photo on the back cover. I validate everyone's contribution which has meant so much!

I also would like to thank Michael Bernard Beckwith, the staff at Agape International Spiritual Center, and all of the members of this spiritual community that I am so privileged to be a part of. When I went to the silent meditation retreat at the end of last year, it was during this time that the revelation of writing this book came to be. And through meeting Michael Beckwith and hugging him, not wanting to let go, meeting and picking the brain of Dr. Marissa Pei, who offered her insights and knowledge about her own life and career, and meeting Stephanie, my partner during the shamanic rituals that we went through, it was truly a life-changing experience. I also want to thank my loving wife, Aki, who has been my spiritual partner, friend, and confidante who has supported me throughout this process.

And with everything that has taken place in my life, I am so thankful and blessed for every experience, every opportunity, and every revelation that allowed me to look at myself completely and honestly. These inner reflections, which were my own mirror reflecting back to me all of who I am, were the starting point to true transformation.

Peace and Blessings!

About the Author

Dr. Glen Hong is a Professor, Clinical Psychologist and Certified Life Coach. He is a clinical expert in treating depression and anxiety which he has done for over 20 years and has taught numerous future clinicians in University settings, as well as publishing a national clinical textbook that is used in both the undergraduate and graduate settings throughout the United States.

Dr. Hong's work intersects the components of neuroscience and spirituality that seeks to address and alleviate symptoms of depression and anxiety through your own nervous system. His life work is to help others to use their emotions as their own guide to healing, and to start living the life that they truly want to live. Glen is also the Director of Field Education at Whittier College for the school of Social Work.

CPSIA information can be obtained
at www.ICGtesting.com
Printed in the USA
LVHW012243261022
731638LV00002B/265

9 781913 479893